BEYOND CHANCE AND NECESSITY

Beyond Chance and Necessity

The Limits of Science and the Nature of the Real

Lorna Green PhD

Writers Club Press
New York Lincoln Shanghai

Beyond Chance and Necessity
The Limits of Science and the Nature of the Real

Writers Club Press
an imprint of iUniverse, Inc.

For information address:
iUniverse
2021 Pine Lake Road, Suite 100
Lincoln, NE 68512
www.iuniverse.com

ISBN: 0-595-26493-X

Printed in the United States of America

BEYOND CHANCE AND NECESSITY

The Limits of Science and the Nature of the Real

Preface

We live in a universe hospitable to every being that inhabits it.

How has it come into being, through matter and mechanism, or by wisdom and creative play? At this point, no one knows.

It is important how we think about the universe, for it is how we will think about ourselves, our place in the scheme of things, the possibilities for our lives.

In our time, the difficulties of assimilating consciousness to the brain indicate not just the limitations of the explanatory principles of modern science but a new understanding of the nature of the universe that answers this question.

The four essays in this book are all about the *real* nature of the universe as it reveals itself at and beyond the frontiers of modern science. They are not arranged chronologically in the order of their composition, but according to an underlying development of ideas.

I invite the reader to consider the limits of our present understanding and to go beyond it.

I.

"Beyond Chance and Necessity"

"The mind stabilizes the unstable brain."
—*William James*

*"…understand how great is the darkness
in which we grope and never forget the
natural-science assumptions with which
we started are provisional and revisable
thing."*
—*William James*

Table of Contents—Essay I

3

1.

Introduction*

The philosopher Hegel suggested that the search for truth unfolded in this manner: Mind explored the world about it, forming a world-picture, proceeding on deep, often unconscious assumptions about the fundamental nature of Reality. Mind proceeded in this way until it encountered anomalies, contradictions. At this point, it returned to examine its fundamental assumptions and revised them to accommodate the contradictions. Then it could continue its search.

So it was with classical physics. The world-picture elaborated by Newton had become disturbingly blurred. Einstein revised the basic concepts of space and time, a new, more inclusive picture emerged, and the search could go on.

---

* Since my graduate studies in the life sciences, I have been dissatisfied with their explanatory principle, Chance and Necessity. This paper has been in me for thirty-five years. Recently, a book by Stephen Pinker entitled HOW THE MIND WORKS appeared on the market, just the latest in the attempt to reduce consciousness to the brain. The book is so irritating in its pretensions, it inspired the present work, the grain of sand to form a pearl.

So it is with every scientist in her/his laboratory.

Physics has changed its nature since classical times. Not so, biology. Modern technology has made it possible to see more and more deeply into the fine structure of matter, but its basic principles remain little changed from the classical formulation by Descartes and others. The progress in bioscience has been steady, continuous.

The belief of most biologists is that biological phenomena are ultimately reducible to physics and chemistry.

The philosopher Whitehead thought that one day biology would revolutionize physics.

Perhaps that day is here. At the forefront of bioscience are appearing anomalies, data that simply cannot be accommodated to scientific materialism. Specifically, *consciousness* is resisting assimilation to the brain.

Descartes first formulated the Mind/Brain dualism: Human beings are composed of minds and bodies, which interact in the pineal gland. Modern researchers in this field, Stephen Pinker, Roger Penrose, Gerald Edelman, and many others, hope to overcome this dualism by showing how the brain produces mind, or consciousness.

My contention is: It cannot be done, for reasons I set forth in this essay.

Instead, my thesis is that the inability to "reduce" consciousness to the brain suggests not simply a revision of the fundamental explanatory principles of biology—chance and necessity—but a whole new picture of the universe to which, as of yet, modern physics has not yet come, though it is well on the way.

I have been considering these issues all my life, first as a bioscience student at McGill University in Montreal and then as a graduate student at Rockefeller University in New York in the sixties.

From childhood, growing up with a physicist father who taught me all about the universe, I had wanted to come to the very heart of that universe, to know deep down what really made it tick.

At Rockefeller, with the independence of study it permitted, I read everything I could and thought about every aspect of bioscience.

I always kept cards in the pockets of my wrap-around skirts on which to write down questions as they occurred to me; these accumulated in a black box on my desk. I believed, like most scientists then, that the truth of the universe lay in physics and chemistry. Yet when I got down among the molecules, I knew something was wrong. Not only did I not understand the cat any better, I had lost the whole cat on the way down to the molecular domain.

What was wrong?

I took to notebooks to find out, and finally found the reason I was so dissatisfied: All scientific explanations rest on "unexplained unexplainers" in terms of which everything else is explained, but which cannot themselves be explained, or somehow rendered "transparent to intellect." (Aristotle)

The forces were in that position in those days; by now the frontier, the wall against truly knowing what makes the universe tick, has shifted further down.

All this ultimately provoked a life crisis that lasted a few years.

Following my graduation from Rockefeller (PhD 1965), I turned to the study of philosophy for answers. After teaching in the great books tradition at St. Johns College in New Mexico for a few years, and deepening into the Western monastic traditions, I took up a wilderness life in Canada's maritime province of Nova Scotia (at age forty-one). There I brooded and contemplated the nature of Reality against all the learning I took in during the first half of my life. (I shall write another time about the joy of living close to the Earth on a daily basis in a practical hands-on way while at the same time raising for myself the great questions of science and philosophy.)

Gradually, answers came.

Recently, I returned to read the latest work in this field.

The essay which follows is a partial answer to what I found out, just an aspect of Truth. The issues I discuss in this paper, the matter/consciousness "joint" in the universe, is the true frontier of bio-science, and what we do with it may have radical implications for the way we live on this planet, for everything we do is underlain by ideas.

I ask that you read my essays, their critiques, their proposals, with an open mind. In this essay, and another to follow, I put forth some of what I have come to know of that universe in which we live and move and have our being.

And yes, I have finally come to the heart of the universe in the everyday lived life.

What I am going to present in these two essays is a *physical* hypothesis about the nature of the universe that should eventually be able to be empirically tested and evaluated.

The first essay, *"Beyond Chance and Necessity,"* deals with the inadequacy of the explanatory principles of modern science to account for anomalies occurring at the consciousness/matter interface; it revises basic assumptions of the life sciences about the relationship between brain and mind. This essay is really a long dialectical inductive argument ascending through a critique of first principles up to a vision of the nature of the universe similar to Plato's ascent to the Forms. (Dialectical argument is really a "laying bare," an analysis, a dissection.)

My theory is spelled out in the second essay, *A New Theory of the Universe,* and then applied to solve the problem of dualism. Many implications follow for the lives of human beings in the world, for science, and for philosophy.

The first essay takes the "ascending path" to a vision of the universe, the second, the descending path back to deal with issues in the world.

Now: A note about method.

All my writing unfolds from the first line, as the universe unfolds, as a flower unfolds in the spring. My favorite way of writing is simply to *state* what I see/have learned/discovered and ask whether you can see it too. Put your eye to my telescope. I write in the first person as a statement about verification. Philosophers like arguments *to* the idea; scientists are more interested in testable implications; people who are neither appreciate clarity. For the sake of my readers, I have returned to my work to give it structure and form in trying to make clear the various theses. May you find it intelligible.

I welcome all questions and discussion about these issues.

2.

Philosophical Background

Over two thousand years ago, the philosopher Plato distinguished between two major principles for explaining the universe. Either it came to be by "art," or by "chance and necessity."[1]

Chance and Necessity was the major explanatory principle of the pre-Socratic scientists of Plato's day. It has always been the principle of science, and it is the explanatory principle of the modern life sciences. The world, the universe, come to be by "*chance* interactions of the atomic parts," and a *necessary* reaction due to the properties of the participants.

Plato chose "by Art." He thought the world patterned after Ideas—unchanging and eternal Forms reassembling the pure objects of geometry—perfect squares, circles, triangles. He thought that only a world fashioned "by Art" had a place for mind, for reason, for virtue, for ethics.

The Forms were glimpsed by the aspirant after a long intellectual flight upwards by the critique of first principles or assumptions. One grasped the Forms as something beyond all principles and assumptions.

The tradition of the philosophers by and large follows Plato. There is intelligence in the universe.

Even early physics followed Plato: The laws of nature were "ideas in the mind of God."

But God was soon dropped. When the Emperor Napoleon, viewing Laplace's mechanical model of the universe, asked, "But where is God"? Laplace replied, "Sire, I have no need of that hypothesis."

And at the present time, the "laws of nature" are a description of the functional relationships of matter.

Matter and mechanism, *chance* and *necessity*, rule our day.

*   *   *

Modern scientists are seldom interested in their philosophical underpinnings, but modern science owes most to the philosopher Descartes.

People before Descartes wrestled with the problem of classification, what to leave in and what to leave out of scientific inquiry.

Descartes simplified it all in one master stroke: The whole of Reality contains just two "Substances," *Mind* and *Matter*. God and human beings alone had *Mind*; everything else, the universe, the Earth and all her inhabitants, were *Matter*.[2]

And what was Matter?

Simply: The weighable, the extended in space and time, devoid of qualities, feelings, thoughts, interior life. Descartes' followers went about kicking dogs, just to hear them howl, reasoning that their howls were not caused by feelings of pain but were merely a function of the wiring of the machinery.

Nature has been viewed that way ever since, the weighable, the extended in space and time, devoid of inner life or intelligence. The universe, the Earth, evolution, all function "blind."

And human beings are rapidly being reduced to the same.

        *   *   *

"Chance and Necessity" rules the day in the life sciences. Francis Crick's work on genetics a few years back was entitled CHANCE AND NECESSITY, and Stephen Pinker's recent book, HOW THE MIND WORKS,[3] refers to the same principle. This principle may be useful in scientific explanation, but it is being elevated to the status of a worldview and pervades all aspects of modern life.

Now, let us begin our steep ascent to a vision of the Real by dialectical argument. My argument contains eight major theses.

My *first thesis* is that "Chance and Necessity," *the* principle of explanation of the life sciences, is really a principle of interpretation, an *assumption* that this is the way the universe works. It is time to change this assumption.

CHANCE AND NECESSITY is a principle of interpretation supplied by the mind. My argument is simply that it is there, in every explanation and cannot be verified. All we see are cause and effect. It is not "proven by any facts," it is an assumed principle which is used to interpret the facts, and explain them—and it is widely invoked today to explain the order, the "apparent" intelligence everywhere in the universe. The facts only seem to bear out that this is the correct explanatory principle. There has been, up until now, a "right fit" between principles and facts which has convinced us that this is the way the universe really is.

The tremendous success of modern science, and modern technology, seems to vindicate the truth of this principle of explanation in the life sciences.

However, there are some signs, in the progress of science, that the outlines of the world picture, the universe picture, which have been drawn up using this principle, are becoming disturbingly blurred.

P implies Q, if not Q then not P. When the fundamental principles of modern science cannot explain things, it is time to change them.

The principle has already *been abandoned* in physics in favour of tele-ological principles, in one form—"the universe was designed with us in mind," and in another—"the universe was expecting us." This about-face of physics has had absolutely no effect whatever on evolutionary theory, which is the custodian of "how we got from there to here," nor on any of the other sciences.

There are anomalies appearing. Basically, in taking "matter" to be all there is—the weighable and extended in space and time, devoid of intelligence—we are actually looking at "the outer of an inner" whose explanatory principles lie elsewhere.

Let me explain.

           *   *   *

The real issue is *Intelligence* and *Purpose.* For the mechanists, intelligence in us, in evolution, in the universe, is only "apparent," the external showing of "chance and necessity"—chance interaction, necessary reaction; chance mutation, natural selection. That is how this pervasive principle deals with the phenomenal realities, among which we "live, and move, and have our being." Purposive behaviour is only apparently so. The universe is blind, and so is evolution.

No wonder human beings are so ill at ease in the universe. *We* are the *only* beings who can function by plans and purposes, and we got here by chance.

And now we are at our first stumbling block—*us.*

Descartes, at least, kept the mind. Some there are who would "reduce the mind to the brain" and our plans and purposes to a function of the wiring of the machinery.

So let us consider *us,* ourselves, the human. Modern science has limits, and nowhere are they more evident and obvious than when we try to explain ourselves, and in particular, *the Mind*

That the universe can be explained by the principle of "chance and necessity" is an *assumption* of modern science. The modern world holds startling indications to the contrary. Perhaps in our time, this most significant turning point in history where Truth is showing itself with greater clarity, we may be able to evaluate the appropriateness of this principle of "chance and necessity" for explaining reality.

So I begin with *us*. I shall also be laying bare other modern assumptions, so well camouflaged that they are taken to be fact.

3.

The Limits of Science

Modern science, despite its status as an all-pervasive world-view of modern times, has limits. My *second thesis*—again a kind of argument for the limits of Chance and Necessity as an explanatory principle—is that *science has limits*. They are to be found in the method itself. A simple analysis will suffice to show this.

These limits originate in science's standpoint on nature, as a spectator of the outsides of things. We have no access to the true inner of things.

Nowhere is this clearer than in the case of human beings. All we see of others are faces, hats and coats going by the window. Is there anything happening within?

Yet this is the stance of the neurophysiologist to the brain. All he sees is grey matter. All he sees, when he puts in his electrodes, is a train of electrical patterns, brain waves.

The patient, meanwhile, is visualizing, is "seeing inwardly," e.g., a horse running along a railway track toward an oncoming train.

If the patient never said a word, never reported to the neurophysiologist that she was seeing this image, the neurophysiologist would not even have suspected the existence of such.

As it is, human beings have a rich interior life of feelings and thoughts, memories, images and reflections. All these things we call mind, or the contents of consciousness, which is completely unlike the matter, the nerves and neurons of the brain which are thought to be "producing" all this.

This is consciousness. It is what Descartes meant by "mind," to be found only in human beings and God.

My *third thesis* concerns another assumption of modern science: Consciousness "appears" only when matter reaches a certain "stage of complexity" in the human, and only in the human. This assumption, too, is an article of faith held so firmly by modern scientists that otherwise it is never questioned. There is no *proof* for this; it derives from a spectator's standpoint.

Curiously, this is a remnant of *Scripture* appearing in modern science: Human beings alone are made in the image and likeness of God, nothing else—no other creature is.

In modern science, the assumption that consciousness exists only in us is a limit of the spectator's standpoint. We do not know whether the "higher animals" have consciousness in there, because they do not tell us about it. In all other respects, they are like us—complex grey matter, electrical activity—but we have no access to the inner.

This is the limitation of the scientific approach to the whole universe: Everywhere, we are the spectator of outsides.

So, because we have no access to the inner, except in ourselves, the tendency has been to say: *It isn't there.* Animals are just weighable and extended in space. And so: A "chance and necessity" universe in which we are a cosmic accident.

Up until now, it has been useful not to have to deal with the inner. But at this historical turning-point, "we are not at home in our interpreted world."[4] It is time to push back frontiers.

Now: Everything we human beings do is underlain by ideas.

The *Scriptures*, and Descartes, and the modern assumption that consciousness exists only in us, all *separate* us from the animals and from the Earth and may lie behind the tremendous damage we have done to the Earth as well as account for the general uneasiness of many people to living in an Infinite universe. It is time to make connections.

And so, my *fourth thesis* concerns the true nature of the human place in the universe. We human beings indeed have a unique status in the scheme of things, but *not* as the only being in the universe that has consciousness, not at all.

Human beings, part and parcel of the universe, in and of the entire universe and Earth, are the only part of the universe in *which we have access to the inner side of the whole.* We are a privileged place in which we can observe that aspect of the universe from which everywhere else we are screened out by the scientific standpoint as a spectator of outsides.

In ourselves, we find consciousness—thoughts, feelings, images, ideas, memories.

My *fifth thesis* is an inferential one—consciousness is in all things.

Why is consciousness not the inner of other animals as well? We suspect its existence in "higher animals"; physiologists think dogs dream as we do, they show all the same signs, outwardly.

My argument is first: A modern "principle of continuity." Life sciences and psychology have tended to reduce us to animal status. I want to make a reduction "upwards." Evolution makes us *continuous* with the animals. We are genetically related to them. Their nervous systems are as complex as ours. All speak languages we have not learned to speak, the grey matter of all show complex electrical activity resembling that in our own brain.

Why confine such consciousness to higher animals? As a graduate student at Rockefeller University in the 1960s, I watched a film of a leucocyte stalking a chain of bacteria. The bacteria were in the field, near a red blood cell. The leucocyte entered the field from one corner, paused, and then changed its shape from amoeba-like to a wedge-shape, the broad edge of the wedge toward the bacteria. Then it proceeded toward them with subtle shifts of the leading edge of the wedge, as if triangulating upon the bacteria. The leucocyte reached the bacteria and formed itself into an amoeba again, and tried to engulf the chain. The bacteria moved in the liquid, so the leucocyte finally backed the bacteria up against the red blood cell and there, proceeded to ingest them. Throughout this procedure, the leucocyte looked like a dog or a wolf stalking its prey. Leucocytes, too, are genetically related to us, our first cousins here, in continuity with us.

Our images and ideas seem to be associated with the electrical properties of the brain. But electrical activity is a property of all living cells, and the whole of an organism can be regenerated from any part. No one form of living material can be deemed more "complex" than any other.

Any living cell is as sophisticated in its own way as the whole organism. I propose to you that cells, too, have consciousness.

And that so do molecules, clever little electrical beings that they are.

In short, modern matter is a long way from Newton's billiard balls. I want to suggest that *matter*, no matter how "complex," will never produce consciousness as the liver produces bile, in us alone, but that the inner-side of all matter is consciousness. Not as sophisticated as ours perhaps, not quite like ours, but consciousness nevertheless, adapted for the niche in which any being finds itself.

Evolution makes us continuous with the atoms. Consciousness would not be in us if it were not in the atoms. Consciousness of some kind is simply the inner side of matter, to be found everywhere matter is, running as it were, in parallel with it. There is absolutely no way that matter would otherwise produce consciousness. Animal "instincts" are simply the "habits of matter" that a species has learned/acquired adapting here. (Whitehead)

This is cosmic dualism, and it makes modern scientists uneasy.

It means that consciousness permeates the universe. Learning is so bound up with our consciousness, it may be a function of all. And learning has been proposed to be able to affect and alter the process of evolution.

The "chance and necessity" universe is growing fuzzy around its edges, for far from being a vast machine, functioning "blind," filled with animals and plants and human beings also functioning "blind," it seems to be something very different indeed, more like a living organism than a mechanical device, and living organisms appear to be more than mechanisms.

That, for the reasons given, is my first claim about consciousness in its relationship to matter. Consciousness is in all beings; it is only our limitation as spectator of the rest of Reality that keeps us from knowing this directly. But we are the keys to the nature of the whole, of which we are an integral part, and by inference, we can assume it is in everything else too.

4.

Reducing Consciousness to the Brain

Now, to further explore the relationships between matter and consciousness, or the brain and consciousness. My *sixth thesis* concerns the attempt made by Stephen Pinker to "reduce" consciousness to the brain, and it is an exposition.

Many are not satisfied with this dualism; they want a unity of reality. And so there is a widespread attempt among both philosophers and scientists to "reduce the mind to the brain." Would it not be wonderful if we could declare the universe nothing but a vast sea of matter? This is the project of materialism.

Consciousness there is, to be sure, but it is simply an "epiphenomenon," very interesting, but not really real; it is the *brain* which does the work. As William James, summing up this position in the nineteenth century, put it: "The mind is to the brain like the shadow of the runner which runs beside him, but never influences his stride."

Stephen Pinker made this attempt is in HOW THE MIND WORKS. "The mind simply *is* the *state* of the molecules, the "computational organs of the brain."(p. 21) My thesis is that the case is not this simple.

First, distinctions will not depart for saying it is so.

The image of a goat standing by a railway track waving a red flag is a very different kind of a thing from molecules or a "state of the molecules."

As Arthur Lovejoy put it for perception in THE REVOLT AGAINST DUALISM: "A train of electrical impulses passes into the brain and there gives rise to something completely unlike them, an idea."[5]

Lovejoy defined the most basic knowing which we have lost sight of in the complexities of this age, as the "getting reported of one thing in a time and a place, as being at that time and place where it is, at another time and place," i.e. remembrance. Few of us can appreciate any more just how miraculous this really is. This is sometimes called the intentionality of ideas.

(Lovejoy concluded that the revolt against Cartesian dualism which has lasted from the seventeenth century to our own day, and included both Bertrand Russell and Alfred North Whitehead, has failed.)

Images and states of molecules, ideas and states of molecules, are two very different kinds of things. If images and ideas have no real function, then, in the great economy of nature, given Occam's razor, what are they doing there at all?

Second, what has to be accounted for is the status of ideas. If this is a mere epiphenomenon of brain activity, what are they there for? Entertainment?

We live our lives by ideas. If they have no real function, why do we spend so long trying to get them clear, why do we argue so fiercely over them, why do we come apart at the seams if we lose our world-views?

If ideas are "states of the molecules," likewise "arrangements of molecules" are a function of ideas. As William James put it: "The mind stabilizes the unstable brain, and the use of strong ideas, the use of reason, strengthens the whole person."

Third, causality between brain and mind appears to be two-way. The widespread use today of mind-altering drugs, which do their work at molecular levels, is one argument for claiming the real work, the real causality is the brain. Yet Bernie Segal gets people out of depression and off serious drugs like Prozac by simply telling them a very different account of the universe than the life sciences' "chance and necessity" account.

The mind/brain interaction would appear to be a two-way street: The mind can influence the brain; the brain can influence the mind. Ideas affect the brain, the brain affects ideas.

Fourth, it is not just the status of ideas that must be accounted for, but the sense of identity we all have, that we are an "I Am," something more than our minds, someone who "sees images and concepts," in the mind. As I write, I am aware of two realities: Outwardly, I see a still room; inwardly, I "see," am aware of, images which have a life of their own and which function quite differently from objects in the outer world. Nor do they resemble outer objects; they are much more beautiful and radiant, like dreams or visions.

How did they get there? What are they doing there?

And who is this "I"?

The pundits like to call this "the ghost in the machine," hoping to get rid of mind and self by ridicule and name-calling.

It will not work. Materialism is a failure, the universe contains something other than "states of molecules," and, except for modern physiologists, this "other" is our own sense of self and soul. It is our interior life of images, thoughts, dreams, reflections, memories, *ideas,* that makes human life meaningful, and possibly, animal, plant, amoebic, and molecular life also.

My *seventh thesis*, an empirical one, is that consciousness is not reducible to the brain but is entirely separable from it.

There is one decisive experience occurring in modern times which is the death-knell for all forms of materialism, scientific or otherwise— the near-death experiences being made with increasing frequency on so many cardiac wards.

The phenomenon is this: Patients with cardiac arrest, who suddenly become "clinically dead" (all vital signs at zero) and are subsequently revived, report finding themselves out of their bodies, hovering near the ceiling, watching the doctors below working on them. They hear all that is being said and are able to read instrument dials which they could not have seen from their beds. When they are revived, they find themselves in their bodies again and are able to report to the doctors all that they saw and heard. (THE NEAR-DEATH EXPERIENCE, Bruce Greyson and Charles Flynn)[6]

What do these experiences, this "experimentum crucis" confirmed by all the necessary verifying perceptual data of science, tell us? Let me do an exegesis of the meaning of these experiences.

First: The essential sense of self, the "I Am," is not tied to the body, but is *separable* from the body. As far as the patient is concerned, "he or she was at the ceiling, looking down on their own body."

Second: Individual consciousness is separable from the body. Whether it requires the body to mature to its present state is another question, but in the person making this experience—even children—consciousness is separable from the body and separable from the brain. It is fully functional in this separated state. The body in the bed is brain-dead, but the mind is fully awake, alive, and alert. So much for Pinker and the computational theorists!

Third: We can see without eyes, hear without ears, think without brains, and remember all that was said.

Fourth: It would appear, if this consciousness never returned to the body, that the patient would then "die." Where would she go? What would happen to her? The far side of these experiences do not concern me immediately.

These "experiments" suggest that we are *essentially* spirit, as religious tradition has always maintained, whatever our ultimate connection with the body may be said to be. Pinker's assumption—*and it is an assumption* or a faith—that the mind *is* the brain, is untenable. His book should be entitled HOW THE BRAIN WORKS. That the mind is a product of the brain is a simple article of scientific faith and cannot be sustained. Pinker's fancy footwork, the pages and pages of experiments, simply obscure the fact that his own principles cannot explain anything more than the principles of those positions he criticizes. Indeed, in the final pages of his book, he admits that with the principle of "chance and necessity," he cannot explain freedom, ethics, or consciousness. Time then, to abandon those principles!

The physicist Feynman made an out-of-body experience in a sensory deprivation tank. He found himself hovering above his body connected by a slender cord. When he willed to raise his left arm, the left arm below him in the tank raised.

I have not been able to find the full account of his reactions to this experience, but he is reported to have said, "I didn't see no (sic) laws of physics being violated."

But what a strange phenomenon. Even the *will* is separable from the body, is non-physical yet able to affect the physical at a distance. What is the whole self? Two "substances" interacting in the navel. Descartes had them interacting in the pineal gland.

We can conclude something else from this experiment: That all our real powers and sense of self lie in something non-physical, invisible, separable and in this case *separated* from the physical, the body.

This is a revolutionary experiment for the life sciences, an *experimentum crucis*. It is their first encounter with spirit. Physics, which is far ahead of the life sciences in revising outworn assumptions, encountered it with *light*.

In view of this experiment which is the death-knell for all forms of materialism, life sciences, like the physical sciences, need to examine what other assumptions they are making about the universe and to recognize that they *are* assumptions. The near-death experiences tell us it is time to be bold. It is time to radically revise our conception of the universe, and our world picture.

My *eighth thesis*, based on these considerations about consciousness and the brain, is that because all the motor powers of human beings lie in consciousness, because consciousness is everywhere, that *consciousness*, and not matter is the essential stuff of the universe. Matter is simply consciousness "stepped down." This is my final argument in our ascent to a true vision of the universe. Now, gentle reader, read on.

5.

The Data to Be Accounted for by Any World-View

The "Chance and Necessity" account of the universe is becoming blurred about the edges. Yet some there are who think it can be our world-view.

If "Chance and Necessity" is to form the basis of the pervasive world-view that it does in modern times, and as Stephen Pinker hopes it will, let us be quite clear about what must be accounted for, "the data," as it were.

I have mentioned the "apparent intelligence in the universe." Reflecting on this, the astronomer, Sir James Jeans remarked early in the 20th century that the universe was beginning to look more and more like a "vast idea" than a "vast machine." Not so for Pinker and the life scientists.

Ethics needs to be explained. Ethics, which often entails self-sacrifice, may well serve the species, but Socrates, awaiting the hemlock in prison, employed ethics as another standpoint on the universe besides the spectator standpoint of Greek science and turned the tables on Anaxagorean materialism: "By Heaven, my legs would have been in Megara by now, given their idea of what was best, did I not consider it more 'right and fitting' to stay here and endure my punishment ordered by the state." People caught in ethical dilemmas experience at least two principles in conflict. To explain a person's ethical decisions, one invokes not the causes of physiology, nor the considerations of "survival value," but other reasons altogether. (See my THE VERIFICATION OF META-PHYSICAL THEORIES: ETHICS AS BASIS OF METAPHYSICS)[7]

A third datum which has to be accounted for by "chance and necessity" proponents is Jung's observations of startling *synchronicities,* "chance" in the modern universe, but too improbable to be "mere chance."

Briefly: As a patient was walking up a forest path with Jung, narrating to him her dream of a night before about a fox, a fox came out of the woods and trotted along the path before them.

Or: A woman was recounting to Jung a dream about a scarab beetle, and the nearest equivalent of a Swiss scarab beetle came tapping at the window. At that point, the patient's resistance to therapy melted.

Jung recognized synchronous events as a kind of "meaningful causality," the significance of which he did not understand. Certainly, for Jung, a pioneer in the understanding of the psyche, it seemed to him to be a form of guidance, a sign that he was "on the right track," and he guided his life by synchronicities. (See Carl Jung's MEMORIES DREAMS AND REFLECTIONS for numerous examples).[8]

How can there be either "guidance" or "signs" in a "chance and necessity" universe, though many people sense such in their lives?

How learning alters all explanatory pictures needs to be taken account of. If this affects evolution, can we still subscribe to "chance and necessity" as explanatory principles of the evolutionary process? And what about the universe itself?

One needs to explain how it is that when an elementary particle is split, one half seems to know what the other half is doing. We need to account for variety, the "playfulness of evolution," producing not just one angler-fish, but dozens of different kinds.

We need to account for beauty. We need to account for the variety on the human scene, for what people are doing in monasteries.

How is it that *prayer works*? In the Benedictine and Charismatic Monastery of Pecos, New Mexico, I witnessed people cured of many maladies, simply by being prayed over by a loving community. Indeed, "the blind see, the lame walk." (Jesus of Nazareth)

We need to account for the widespread belief in reincarnation in almost every major world religion.

We need to account for the fact that many people are not at home in our "interpreted world," for the instinct to praise, for the fact that so many people outside the scientific community believe in "God," a creator.

We need to account for the emotions and especially for the sense of the holy, "*mysterium fascinans et tremendum.*" (Rudolph Otto) We need to account for the widespread "New Age" phenomenon of channelling entities from other realms of the universe, other, non-physical realms of the universe.

In fact, the whole modern scene needs to be accounted for.

And it can be.

The modern technological world, with its ethic, "if it can be done, do it," is the off-spring of the materialism, mechanism, and the explanatory principles of "chance and necessity." We are a scientific century, and the unprecedented achievements of modern science seem to confirm its explanatory principles as being true.

My thesis is that for the successes of modern mechanistic science, Cartesian science, life sciences, we are paying a high price, and the negative results are like the negative result of an experiment we have been conducting for the past three hundred years, as modern science has gained ascendancy.

Consider what they are: The incredible pressures of the workplace; more and more work for less and less pay; the frantic pace of modern work; the fact that the corporations regard the entire population as merely a workforce of slaves; that we are slaves to our machines; that we simply have no principles by which to evaluate what is happening to us. We are a giant locomotive running the wrong way down the tracks.

Nowhere is this clearer than in the case of the Earth. As I have argued elsewhere (EARTH AGE: A NEW VISION OF GOD, THE HUMAN, AND THE EARTH, 1994), the crisis on the Earth is the negative result of all our scientific and philosophical traditions of thinking and calls that thinking into question. [9]

As a world-view, "chance and necessity" has little to offer about the "meaning of life." The Victorians were so inwardly bankrupt that they clung to private morality. Our age is so inwardly impoverished that people cling to work. They die, no longer "satisfied with life," as did so many of our ancestors. They die "tired of life." (Ludwig Edelstein) Perhaps the widespread experience of depression and the need for psychiatrists is simply a function of believing in the principles of "chance and necessity," a meaningless life in a meaningless universe.

Again, we are the keys to the whole.

We are a *part* of the universe we are explaining, and if our explanatory principles, powerful as they are, bankrupt our lives and inner beings, that may be a sign that something is wrong with the explanatory principles. We are the test of our principles.

That is to say: The effects of believing in those principles—our whole life is dependent on our ideas—on those who believe them may be a way of arguing against them.

"God" is no alternative at this point. Modern religions are in as much disorder as the modern world. Nor can "God" come just shot from the pistol. If we end up there, we must end up there with "no leaps and no losses." (Hegel)

I am going to propose something new. None of facts to be accounted for, taken alone, is definitive in itself, but taken together, they suggest that the "chance and necessity" world-view is false.

It is time for a change, before we lose what is left of our humanity.

In the essay to follow, *A New Theory of the Universe*, I present a theory of the nature of things which is wholly new to modern science if not completely new to philosophers. Both essays appear in a shortened version in *The Journal of Speculative Philosophy, 2003.*

6.

References

[1] Plato, THE LAWS, COMPLETE WORKS, Cooper, E. and D. Hutchinson, (eds.) Hackett Pub. IN 1997.

[2] Descartes, R., MEDITATIONS, University of Notre Dame Press IL 1992.

[3] Pinker, S., HOW THE MIND WORKS, W.W. Norton and Co. NY 1999.

[4] Rilke, R.M., DUINO ELEGIES, #9, University of California Press CA 1961.

[5] Lovejoy, A., THE REVOLT AGAINST DUALISM, Open Court IL 1960.

[6] Greyson, B. and C. Flynn, THE NEAR-DEATH EXPERIENCE, Charles C. Thomas IL 1960.

[7] Green, L., THE VERIFICATION OF METAPHYSICAL THEORIES: ETHICS AS BASIS FOR METAPHYSICS, Interface Press NS 1989.

[8] Jung, C.G., MEMORIES DREAMS AND REFLECTIONS, Random House NY 1989.

[9] Green, L., EARTH AGE: A NEW VISION OF GOD, THE HUMAN AND THE EARTH, Paulist Press NJ 1999.

II.

A New Theory of the Universe:
How The Mind Really Works

"Nowadays when they apply Occam's razor, they shave away half the face with the beard."

—*Emil Fackenheim*

Table of Contents—Essay II

1.

Introduction

In the previous essay, *Beyond Chance and Necessity*, I claim that consciousness is in all things, not simply in the human, and drew the necessary implications of the near-death experiences being made on so many cardiac wards: That consciousness in the human is separable from the body.

The "chance and necessity" explanatory principle is simply inadequate for explaining the universe which includes near-death experiences; yet some there are who would elevate this principle to the status of a comprehensive world-view.

In the first essay, I laid out just some of the marvelous phenomena on the Earth-plane that such a world-view would account for. The job cannot be done by the principle of chance and necessity.

In this paper, I propose a new, alternative view of the universe by a simple reinterpretation of the nature of energy: All energy has consciousness, all consciousness has energy.

Here, then, is the account of the universe that everywhere has consciousness as its inner side.

This new view is elaborated, and on its basis, the mind-body problem of Descartes and scientific dualism is solved.

In addition, I spell out many of the implications of the new theory of the universe—for us, modern civilization, life on Earth.

2.

A New Theory of the Universe

Physicists resort to field properties, and an ever-renewed apprecia-tion and awe for the Mysteries of the universe is on the increase among them. They seem to have left the life sciences far behind.

Thus, for modern physics, what is real is not matter, it is energy, and the entire universe, and all in it, is part of a vast energy field. Matter has disappeared, at the lower limits, in favour of, what?

In favour of vibration. Matter is formed by vibrations in an energy field.

With "energy," we are at the same limits as matter, no insight into "inners." Energy: The ability to do work. What does the work? (Tom Berry). Is there any other standpoint than the scientific standpoint as the "spectator of outsides"?

I mentioned our selves. In ancient times, and again in modern, there was a very different standpoint taken on the universe: Meditation.

The Rishis of India spent their lives in meditation, as did the Buddhists. As the Buddha put it, "The conditioned, temporal, finite" rests on "the unconditioned, eternal, infinite."

The Rishis concluded that the entire universe is formed of consciousness.

The physiologist would say these men are just examining their own inner and cannot learn anything from that beyond what has been said here.

Not so fast, men of science; the psyche is not in space as the brain is. It is not bound, as matter is. It opens inwardly into the hidden webwork of the universe. I want to say a little more about consciousness.

The only place we can really examine consciousness is in ourselves. We can experience it, as we experience our selves, for it is too fundamental to be defined. We are it.

And I want to say that it is more than thoughts and images. It is the dark matrix which contains them, as one thinker has put it, "the space between thoughts." Could this not be the very matrix of the entire universe? I have proposed that the continuity of evolution implies that consciousness is in all beings.

With "near-death experiences," we saw that consciousness was separable, and could be separated from the body, and that the major aspects of seeing, hearing, thinking and willing were in a conscious, separated self.

Now, let us challenge the assumption of physics that "energy is all there is." My thesis is that the inner of matter is consciousness; the inner of energy is consciousness. All energy has consciousness, all conscious-ness has energy. That is the universe.

So: We are now ready for a new theory of the universe.

The near-death experiences gave us the clue: All the true explanatory principles of the universe lie in the within of things. (Teilhard de Chardin)*

I am proposing, not a dualistic, but a new unity view of the universe: The unique, One, being formed of consciousness.

This is to flip the priorities of modern science 180 degrees. The uni-verse comes to be, not out of matter, but out of consciousness. Consciousness is the independent variable, matter is the dependent variable. Matter is an elaboration of consciousness. The brain is the physical manifestation of mind in the physical realm. The physical is actually a very limited part of the true universe, which is primarily

---

* I realize that I am not the only person to quarrel with the reductive approach of modern science, its explanatory principle of "chance and necessity," and with the *wholly* inadequate models for the relationship of consciousness and brain. Many philosophers, psychologists, biologists and anthropologists have criticized them, and certainly modern physics is in the process of entirely rewriting our notions of causal-ity. Nor am I the only thinker to propose that consciousness is the real essence of the universe. Among the ancients, Thales, the first recorded philosopher who claimed that "all is water," may have been using water as a metaphor for consciousness which, like water, knows no real boundaries. See also Anaxagoras—"Mind arranges all things"—and Heraclitus—"Listening not to me, but to the Logos, it is wise to agree that all things are one." Now, in our modern century, we have an experiment which proves them right. *Genesis*, Plato, Kant (though in a different way) and Hegel also give prior-ity to mind in the universe. I have not quoted modern philosophers because I simply wanted to give my own version of the truth.

spiritual. The effect of drugs on the mind is to interfere with our connection with the mind, not with the mind itself. The mind precedes
birth and survives after death. When parts of the brain are missing, full
consciousness cannot incarnate.

The universe is essentially a consciousness universe, and all its form-
ative powers and principles, its intelligence, its wisdom, are in consciousness. Matter is the outer shell, the real epiphenomenon here, an
elaboration of consciousness, which is not just within it but goes far
beyond it.

Feynman, that most inquisitive of physicists, unafraid to challenge
his assumptions, put the matter this way: "Maybe the whole thing is
wrong."

Well, it is not wrong; it is just partial, mapping only the outsides of
the universe.

We have a unified concept of reality now, not the principle of "chance
and necessity," but Plato's "by Art." The universe is primarily spiritual
rather than material. What of explanatory principles? Those of the life
sciences are really descriptions, not explanations. The new, true
explanatory principles lie within consciousness. Creation originates in a
vast "sea of love-consciousness" (we can speak only metaphorically of
these things) criss-crossed by "vibrations." These vibrations have frequency and intent, and the need to create, and are wholly loving, devoid
of fear. Like-vibrations "dance together to see what they can make." The
entire universe emerges through "creative play" rather than mechanism.

Bundles of vibrations, all endowed with love and intent, form *Ideas* which are thus intermediaries between the very foundations of things and the manifested world.

These ideas are different from Plato's—they are conscious, loving and endowed with the intent to manifest, and they change, witness the world. Matter arises where ideas interact with the vibration that is the human and other beings. Nor do they require a half-god to translate them into "world," but they harmoniously manifest themselves. Consciousness must create.

The universe is a consciousness universe.

What came "before" the Big Bang?

What exploded?

The consciousness of God, finding its way to incarnate itself in physical form.

"Let there be Light."

And who is God?

Infinite Consciousness.

Infinite Consciousness, best referred to as Spirit, for its invisibility to our senses.

And, it is a love-consciousness at that. Fear is only a function of the separation experienced in the physical plane. We are all essentially lovers here. There is a whole continuum of consciousness ranging from atoms and molecules to God. Infinite Consciousness is in each of us, and every plant and animal, every stone and star, is a portion of that consciousness in a body.

Diagrammatically, this universe looks like this:

Spirit (God, Infinite Consciousness)
|||
Ideas (Consciousness)
//|||\\
World
\\|||//
Us

This diagram is rough at best, for in the spiritual world, Oneness prevails.

The Ideas are an intermediary, intermediate stage of organization between the pure "sea of love-consciousness" criss-crossed by vibrations together and us, an organization of vibrations. Where do fundamental particles go when then disappear? Back into the "sea of consciousness" whence all of Creation originates. This "sea of consciousness" may be what physicists are now calling the "dark energy of space."

And God is an "Idea" so powerful that it affects every other idea and every thing that emerges from Ideas.

Truly, we live our lives in the shadow of ideas.

How many dimensions does the universe have? For physical accounts, this was a problem. Five? Eleven? In consciousness, the universe has infinite dimensions and is far grander and more magnificent than anything we have hitherto imagined.

Now, that is the picture of the universe which I have assembled with the help of modern physics, which has reduced everything to energy and vibration.

I have been able to access many of these realities for myself in deep meditation, far beyond the level of mind. The shamans of ancient Mexico, like Don Juan Mateus (Carlos Castaneda) could "see into the sea of consciousness." With meditation one can access any knowledge.

How will this help the life sciences, still stuck in Cartesianism with its "chance and necessity" principle elaborated in the seventeenth century?

They need to know they are missing something.

That they do not *see* everything. That is, that they are missing the motor. In the haste to reduce all things to matter, they are missing the real driving power of the universe—consciousness with its will to create, the true source of motive power.

As a cell biologist, I believed the description of a cell would be complete when the state of the parts were specified in terms of the state of the sub-parts, and these in turn specified in terms of the state of the molecules. That is the conviction of all cell biologists.

When the description is complete, will we be satisfied? I doubt it. We will want to know what really matters, makes all the mechanisms move. We have left out consciousness. Candice Pert's work, MOLECULES OF

EMOTION,[1] claims that much of what has been attributed to the brain happens all over the body. Every cell has consciousness.

As we look at the physical realm, we are looking at a shadow, a marker of the true, invisible event, as then—watching my pigment cells, watching protoplasm—I often caught a gleam of light as consciousness connected with consciousness.

This is my new view of the nature of the universe.

Only consciousness has the capacity to accommodate all the phenomena I have put out. If the modern life sciences and even physics do not realize that consciousness is the essential nature of the universe, then science will end by being merely a handmaid to technology.

Three different phenomena are a different kind of evidence for this new view. First, the channelling phenomenon itself, where one consciousness informs another physical being. Second, the mind/body unity, taken together with near-death experiences which is emerging in modern medicine. And finally, the identity of the observer and the observed in modern physics.

Now, what we have here is a reconciliation among science, philosophy and religion at their intersection. All disciplines have their own valid contributions to make to knowledge.

Before I ask what this startling new view of the universe might mean, I want to cite once more the two philosophers I have been quoting in this work—Descartes at the laying of the foundations of modern science, Plato at the dawn of thought.

Descartes guided his whole life by his vivid dreams. Towards the end of his life, after elaborating his mechanistic view of the universe, he had a dream in which he saw the universe as a vast machine, and in the centre, propelling the whole, was Consciousness.

A prophetic taste of things to come.

The universe is like a living organism, the whole universe is evolving, we ourselves are evolving, God is a living God, and the entire process is shaped by consciousness, intelligence.

Plato, in early Athens, put forth his famous simile of the cave in THE REPUBLIC.[2]

Briefly, human beings live in an underground cave where they are chained by the neck so they can only see the wall in front of them.

A fire lit behind them casts their shadows on the wall, and they take these shadows to be reality, and they compete for prizes in measuring the rates and the shapes of the shadows.

If someone were to come down into the cave, unchain the inhabitants, and turn their heads, they would first see the fire behind them, and understand the true state of things. And then, if they were to be led up the stairs and out of the cave and into the light of day, they would be utterly amazed. At first their eyes would be blinded by the light, but gradually they would make out the shapes of trees, of people and animals walking about, and finally, the sun itself, author of all Being, and they would utterly marvel at the true nature of things. The sun is consciousness, the realities are Ideas. Plato was the only philosopher, followed by Plotinus, to believe in these Ideas.

How much these two men were able to see!

Pinker's book concludes by stating that the answers to questions about the origins of consciousness, free-will and ethics will ever be beyond the power of the human mind. Yes, because consciousness is the most fundamental and essential thing in the universe out of which everything else comes to be, not itself to be explained, but the explanatory principle of everything else. The logical thing for Pinker to do, when his premises have failed to account for the phenomena, is to revise them. And so I propose a new Copernican revolution.

Copernicus set Western science on its present course by making a total reversal of the assumption of his contemporaries that the Earth was the centre of things. Copernicus made a 180-degree flip, to claim not the Earth but the Sun was the centre of things.

We are all at a major turning point into the Third Millennium, a principle of historical grace and truth.

I am inviting modern science and the philosophers who base themselves on it to make another such Copernican revolution, a major paradigm shift, to dethrone matter and energy, and with them "chance and necessity" as the centre of their conceptual universe, and flip 180 degrees to see that consciousness, and not matter and energy, "chance and necessity," is the true foundation of Reality and then begin to determine what follows, and to pose the appropriate new questions.

And that they begin to see the universe, the Earth and the modern world not as they have hitherto seen it, under fallacious principles proposed from limited human perspective in the physical, but as God sees it.

We observe here that consciousness as the essential stuff of the universe is what Roger Penrose is looking for to complete quantum theory, that underlying "something else." The laws of consciousness are not the laws of matter, consciousness travels instantaneously to all locations; consciousness is eternal, timeless. Consciousness has "field" and "particle" properties, organized into ideas or images, or simply imageless substrata which we can explore in ourselves. But it requires that we shift our standpoint completely to "see" this, because physics began with a world of things, the ordinary world of our perception. Its troubles come at the limits of our range—the very small, the very fast, the very far off.

That is where the physicist's principles—classical and modern quantum mechanical—disturbingly blur. The anomalies force us to revise the fundamental assumptions on which science has been proceeding.

The major assumption, because of this predominance of "things" in the physical realm, is that nothing but the physical domain exists and that consciousness only emerges at a certain stage of complexity of the physical.

Plato thought the physical world that we all took for granted was an appearance; reality lay in something more fundamental and "invisible." Kant did also, though for different reasons.

I am claiming that the invisible, but more real, is consciousness. Consciousness is primary here, matter is secondary.

The properties of consciousness are quite different from that of matter, its frozen derivative.

Consciousness is eternal; it is the consciousness of Spirit—Infinite Consciousness—and it is totally continuous with all parts of itself. It mediates to us through ideas. This reversal of assumptions is to stand modern science on its head. And it implies a reduction "upwards." The laws of physics are derivative of the laws of living things, the laws of living things are derivative from the laws of Spirit. Yes, it is time to stand modern science on its head. The Emperor was losing his mind. (Roger Penrose, THE EMPEROR'S NEW MIND)[3]

Indeed, science is already not what it seems: All scientific explanations rest on "unexplained explainers." The forces are in that position today. Familiarity with the use of the term makes us think we know what they are. Are they "pushes and pulls"? Or are they the "mind of the universe"? No one knows what they really are. They are occult entities at the heart of scientific knowledge.

I want to emphasize my continuity with the work of other thinkers.

Among the ancients, Plotinus seems to have understood this.

Among the great philosophers, Spinoza, Leibniz and Whitehead assigned a fundamental role to consciousness. My view is perhaps most similar to Spinoza's ETHICS, "a glorious baroque elaboration of the hypothesis that the universe is a single unified substance with infinitely many aspects interacting in infinitely complicated ways and that God and Nature are just two alternative designations for it." (Jonathan Rea, *London Review of Books*, January 24, 2002)

My difference from Spinoza is that everywhere I can dovetail my theory into experience, to indicate that this really *is* a *true* description of the universe.

Among modern thinkers, Michael Talbot, in THE HOLOGRAPHIC UNIVERSE,[4] has introduced the notion that the whole of the universe is contained in every part.

David Bohm has introduced the theory that there is a deeper, under-lying order to the physical that we do not know anything about yet.[5]

Deepak Chopra, in all of his books, and especially in his tape, "Every Day Immortality," brings together quantum physics and the human self.

Roger Penrose believes that beyond quantum mechanics must lie something else, and I have given it here.

After thinking through the ideas for this paper, I was given the remarkable book by Danah Zohar entitled THE QUANTUM SELF.[6] Her conclusions are strikingly like my own. Beginning from a basis in quantum physics, she develops a quantum mechanical model of the mind, and offers insights into the nature and bases of ethics and free-dom that Pinker's materialism could not as well as into a relational uni-verse with plenty of place for God. She only does not recognize the separability of consciousness from matter and the more fundamental role of consciousness in the universe. But hers is a deeply refreshing work, based on both science and philosophy, although whether Pinker would consider her models to be an *explanation* of free-will, conscious-ness and ethics, is doubtful.

I also recommend THE SELF-AWARE UNIVERSE: HOW CON-SCIOUSNESS CREATES MATERIAL REALITY[7] by the quantum physicist, Amit Goswami, another book which came to my attention after completing these essays. Like me, he proposes consciousness, not matter, is the real "stuff" of the universe and shows how all the paradoxes of modern physics can be explained on this assumption. He also produces a quantum mechanical model for mind.

May this agreement among unrelated thinkers cause you to take our claims seriously!

Paul Davies and John Gribbins come to the same conclusion in THE MATTER MYTH.[8] Let the life scientists take note. Only consciousness can account for all the data and for the richness and interweaving of the world, including its many and varying different philosophies.

3.

How the Mind *Really* Works:
The Solution to Dualism

This essay and the previous one up until now have been a long inductive argument in many steps to the new conception of the universe. Now, let us put this new conception to work to solve ancient problems. My thesis is that with this theory of the universe we can solve the problem of dualism. This is a kind of proof of the theory itself.

I want to propose a conceptual thesis with empirical ramifications.

Descartes formulated dualism in its modern form: Human beings are Minds and Bodies.

Now: Descartes, for the best of reasons, thought the human mind and body interacted in the pineal gland. Let us get specific.

Roger Penrose thinks, for the best of reasons, that the physical basis of mind is the microtubules of the brain, because the bound water can "contain" quantum events. (SHADOWS OF THE MIND)[9]

I have claimed that the whole universe comes to be from consciousness. I want to propose an explanation.

Where does mind, consciousness, which extends beyond the life and death of the brain, "fasten" in?

We are making the assumption that it needs to. I propose another model.

Consciousness is not "attached" to the brain. Consciousness flows through the brain like a fluid.

How to account for the relative stabilities in our consciousness?

Even fluids have stability, especially water in its various forms. And rivers have banks, structures.

How does consciousness interact with the brain? The brain is composed of cells and the cells of the brain drink fluid.

But the question persists, and baffles the mind: How can two such seemingly different kinds of things, consciousness and the grey matter of the brain, interact? After all, the bile secreted by the liver is the same kind of thing as the liver; they are both material. Even Penrose's physical quantum events are very different from an idea, an image. Dualism remains.

The answer is that consciousness and the grey matter of the brain are only seemingly different. At the deepest levels of matter, matter is not dense at all, but is vibrations, waves, the sorts of things that something like consciousness could mesh with. And this is the key to overcoming dualism, at the deepest levels the two different things must be shown to be the same.

And, in fact, the brain at the deepest level is vibrations of consciousness.

This is not to say there is no outer world. Reality is perfectly objective.

It is to say that the dense stuff which manifests to our senses as matter is really formed of dense bundles of consciousness vibrations I have called *Ideas.*

We have, essentially, in ourselves, two different forms of consciousness—one "rarefied," one "highly condensed," interacting.

Our question then becomes: How do Ideas as I have described them interact?

Basically, Ideas are always giving off vibrations. The Ideas in consciousness are bundles of vibration which stimulate the brain, literally aligning the vibrations of the brain so that we pick them up as ideas. Molecular and quantum events are set in motion by vibrations. They, too, are vibrations. Throughout, we are dealing with the same "kinds of things," not "matter" but Ideas. This is the solution of the problem of dualism. At its lower limits, the brain is the same kind of thing as the mind, not the other way around. The brain is like a sensitive antenna for the mind. I am presenting a unity account of Being.

The view of Reality, and the solution of "the problem of dualism" I am proposing is so new I believe it bears more detailed restating and elaborating.

The problem of dualism arose because two completely disparate sorts of things—consciousness and the grey matter of the brain—seem yet able to interact. How do they do it?

Materialists have thought to get rid of the problem by "reducing" the mind to the brain. Their mind is the brain.

This is merely semantics, a play on words, and it will not work. Near-death experiences prove the mind completely separable from the brain. If Francis Crick wants to search for the soul, he will need a stepladder to the ceiling to reach the patient who hovers there, looking down at his brain-dead body on the bed below. The methods of empirical science will avail him little if he would really know the truth of things. (Francis Crick, THE ASTONISHING HYPOTHESIS: SCIENTIFIC SEARCH FOR THE SOUL).[10] "The astonishing hypothesis"—that mind is the brain—is not astonishing at all. It is as old as materialism, and near-death experiences prove it false.

I have taken a different route, through reflection, meditation, converse with the spiritual realm, coming through a lifetime to the true nature of that Reality which "loves to hide," as Heraclitus put it before Plato's time.

I have learned that the foundations of the world we know and take for granted, in which we live and move and have our everyday life, are not matter, not atoms, not quantum events, but Ideas, bundles of "like consciousness vibrations, endowed with love, frequency, and the intent to manifest." They harmoniously manifest themselves, and establish harmonious interactions, and they change, unlike Plato's ideas.

They are the source of all existence. Our physical world arises as the interaction product of our sensory apparatus and brain—with Ideas. Whence the solidity?

It is a function of the "density" of ideas, as we know that the table, solid to our touch, is really mostly empty space.

For this reason, we can say that "physicalness" is a camouflage over the Real, and that the senses, wonderful as they are, are, as one author has put it, "lovely liars." Every purple sunset and golden dawn, each jagged rock and breaking wave, is the product of the interaction of ideas with our senses and brain.

So Plato called the physical world an Appearance. Nor is the physical world self sufficient on its own, as modern science assumes, but it is supported and maintained from deep within the spiritual dimensions of the universe.

Our world is a camouflage over the Real.

We live in a thing-filled world.

But what is so wonderful about our world? The Real shines through it, and through our world of things, and in our daily events, we catch glimpses of it, perhaps while doing the ironing or getting on a bus, or in nature among living things, or while listening to the words of others. The world is more than Cartesian "matter." And it is indeed a magical place to be.

And so we return to dualism, and the resolution of the problem.

The problem is resolved only at the limit of Reality, because, brain and consciousness appear widely disparate in the three dimensional world, but at the lowest level of brain and consciousness we are dealing with the same kinds of things: Consciousness vibrations.

The ideas in consciousness stimulate the brain, aligning the consciousness vibrations of the brain, as a magnet aligns iron filings, or a current in one wire induces a current in another. Ideas thus reproduce themselves in the brain so they can enter into our experience. Molecular and quantum events are set in motion by vibrations. Since quantum events, too, are vibrations, we are dealing with the same "kinds of things." (To some extent the brain can also align consciousness.)

That is what Reality is, and that is the solution of "the problem of dualism." There are not "two kinds of things" in the universe, Mind and Matter, as Descartes maintained. There is only one: Consciousness. At the deepest level, mind and brain share a common structure.

Can anything more be said of alignment? Vibrations align in part by frequency and…

And…

And here we are indeed at the limits of science and of insight into the mystery. The forces between consciousness vibrations are "like electromagnetic forces." It is not by chance that such analogies come to mind, but they are not that, being beyond the domain of the physical. However, electromagnetic events are the first and most fundamental level of the manifestation of consciousness vibrations in the physical.

Here we are in the heart of the mystery. These things the Buddha experienced in a state of enlightenment and was made happy by them. I have been trying to translate into scientific terms what enlightened consciousness knows. And my terms are mechanical. It seems we are in mechanics all over again at a lower level. Not so, but in breaking new ground we have only mechanical models for translation and the categories of our understanding take this form. We are in the domain of oneness, not separation, and we as yet lack ways to speak about it.

What I have sketched, whether "empirically fertile" or not, is how the universe really is. It is complex, but not complicated.

What of the microtubules? My fish pigment cell was full of them, where they seemed to be involved with granule motion. I do not believe microtubules any more involved with these events than any other cell structure. Certainly, the brain does not "produce" consciousness; it only "contains it." Consciousness is bigger than the brain.

And what of the self? An idea-shape.

What can we say of our ideas which we so labour to get clear about? Vibrations of consciousness, having immense power and force, shadows of the real thing, more compact versions of the real thing. Concepts come to us from beyond the camouflage system, when we are ready for them, perhaps when we are worthy of them. We live our lives in the shadow of Ideas.

Gerald Edelman and Giulio Tononi have released the first book on this subject to appear in the new millennium: A UNIVERSE OF CONSCIOUSNESS: HOW MATTER BECOMES IMAGINATION.[11]

Again, these authors assume the brain produces consciousness, gives rise to consciousness, but they never tell us how this happens.

What they do instead is provide two parallel descriptions, a most complex description of consciousness, and one of neuronal activity. In their own words, to explain consciousness is to give the neural process to which it "corresponds."

What they have done is merely restate dualism in a more complicated way. The crucial chapter on Qualia does not even recognize the problem. Again, that the brain produces the mind is a simple article of faith.

Nor do they describe "a universe of consciousness," only human consciousness, which may feel like a universe when you are in it but is not the whole.

Yet the field properties, the great fluxes of neuronal activity, reminiscent of Goswami's tangled hierarchies which carry consciousness, must surely be the case. If this account is put together with the explanation I have given, a total picture begins to emerge.

Consciousness incarnates in the brain, it employs the brain, it uses the brain and builds a self with its own structures of memory, it builds up world-views (and then, when enlightened, it lays them down again). Consciousness flows through the brain, but it is not the brain, and when it leaves, the brain dies.

Edelman and Tononi admit that they cannot really explain the major problems of consciousness with their premises. Time to abandon those materialistic premises; then all will fall into place, and the new questions for research will arise.

At this most fundamental "joint" in existence, that is about all I can say for now. I have been speaking in metaphor. Precise description is yet beyond us, for we are in the realm of oneness rather than the separations of the physical plane. Still we can at least name the universe aright, as I have here. It is essentially a conscious universe, a universe which has consciousness, not a material universe, and perhaps when we are one day free of our bodies, we shall know more.

Portions and hints of these realities can be glimpsed in deep meditation, and daily through the events of our lives. I hope what I have said here may suffice to raise new questions, whether "empirically fertile" or not.

Yes, let the new science of consciousness flourish.

Know that its true scope is nothing less than the entire universe of consciousness in all its various forms, and that essentially, like the forms of water, All is One, as the ancient Socratic mystics such as Thales and Heraclitus intuited.

We are beyond the "chance and necessity" universe, and the universe is more than mechanism.

Before I move on, I want to call attention to Roger Penrose's daring acceptance of Plato's ideal status for number—Plato is the supreme Realist when it comes to Ideas—in an age in which, as his carping critics insist, Platonism is unfashionable. Say rather that this age is out of sorts, missing the mark. Roger Penrose is a pioneer.

Roger Penrose gives Platonic status to number. Plato knew that ideas existed for many other things as well, and I have included them here in a broader context as part of the ways in which consciousness organizes itself.

What I have presented here, as luminous and clear to my inner vision as the outer world is to yours, is a new unity view of Reality.

Can I say what consciousness is?

Yes, I can.

Consciousness is God, on the surface modified by the world, in the depths the real thing. God dwells within you.

It is the pure "dark energy of the universe" in us; one can experience it unmodified by thought or image in meditation. On the surface, in the head, consciousness glows with activity. We form a perfect unity in our depths with a "dark energy of the universe." Only our minds separate us.

I can no longer contemplate these awesome mysteries. Let us therefore move on to some of the implications for our lives here.

4.

Perspective and Implications

My thesis—conceptual, analytic, empirical—is that this new theory, namely that consciousness is the real "stuff" of the universe, will affect every department of human understanding and activity and will radically change the way we perceive and relate to our planet and each other. It will lead to a more open and happy world then the one based on three hundred years of mechanism, separative thinking which has de-divinized and de-sacralized an Earth which was once worshiped as a goddess.

I want to say that many of these theses are autobiographical also, as I have experienced their truth in a wilderness life.

The sciences have a fine tradition of "saving the appearances." Only now, in the zeal of "chance and necessity" theorists and an exotic array of philosophers and scientists, eager to shave theory with Occam's razor, they shave away "half the face with the beard." (Emil Fackenheim)

A "by Art" universe, a universe which originates in consciousness, can account for many more phenomena if it is taken as a world-view, than can "chance and necessity"–this in itself a proof of its truth. I sketch a few of the non-scientific implications here, as suggestions. I doubt that all will find them acceptable, but I think they follow with this reversal of principles. They are, in fact, the corollaries of this new theory. Let us take the descending path from our vision of the universe into its ramifications. This new view can accommodate all the data I specified in my first essay.

There is room for angels, consciousness without physical form, as both medieval and moderns attest. There is room for spiritual universes and spiritual beings which are not embodied in physical life, spiritual guides and guidance.

There is room for Spirit, as all religions have claimed. Indeed, as C.S. Lewis put it: "A road opens up in solitude to a reality so ultimate that it disdains to embody itself in sense."

There is room, in this view of the nature of things, for the real world which includes scientists, meditators and philosophers. All their approaches yield valid knowledge of the universe.

Consciousness knows no real boundaries, unlike matter. All consciousness interacts, as telepathic experiments suggest.

There is room for spiritual worlds, as well as the physical, as Native North Americans, and indigenous people all over the world have maintained—worlds which are purely consciousness, not incarnate in physical form. The left brain was only blocking the view.

God can readily be found, not just "up there in Heaven" but down here, within us and within the Earth, as mystics have always claimed, since all of Reality, all of our "thingy" world, is God under a thousand forms, as the Bhagavad-Gita of ancient India teaches. God also dwells within us; the Self is fathomlessly deep on our inner side.

The whole of Reality is sacred for being formed from the consciousness of God.

It is time to admit animals and plants have consciousness, as every pet owner already knows.

It is time to admit, in studying animals and their behaviour, the principle of this century—"the observer affects the observed"—and become shamans in our effort to know them.

It follows from this account that the Earth and all her inhabitants are living, conscious, spiritual, and divine beings (formed from the Consciousness of God), as spiritual as we are, eager for a relationship with us. We must find new ways of relating to them, not by dissection and analysis, but spirit to spirit, and soul to soul. The conviction of scientists that they are just cleverly wired mechanisms has given us a licence to do them all in. If animals and plants, like us, are conscious, spiritual beings, they too have rights to "life, liberty, and the pursuit of happiness."

The view that consciousness, not matter, is the real "stuff" of the universe opens up new possibilities for us here.

The possibilities for a relationship within our own species and with other species are immense. Animals are always slipping in and out of their bodies, back and forth between the spiritual and the physical worlds.

There are new frontiers for the human too. Far from being merely brains in bodies, as Descartes maintained, we are fragments of God in a body, portions of Infinite Consciousness in a body. What faculties and powers are available for us? The large silent parts of the brain, what secrets do they contain? The psyche, not in space and time quite in the same way as the body is, is quite likely multi-dimensional and gives us access to many worlds other than our own. As an Abbot once put it to me: "All the doors to the spiritual world open on our inner side." A greatly expanded experience is available to us if we will but "put our eye to the telescope," follow the necessary practices.

This may give us some idea of what those who meditate and people in monasteries are doing—opening up to Spirit and the universe through their inner sides.

In our view, all spiritualities must change. The destruction and upheaval in the world, right now, I take to be a function of burying what Jung called "the shadow side," for all religions have emphasized the good, everything else—especially anger, which Catholics made into a deadly sin—was banished to the unconscious where, for being unrecognized, it only gained power and then erupted to be projected upon others and on the Earth.

If we are to have a happy, sane world, we need to be whole and to admit into our consciousness all that we have repressed and buried in the unconscious. We are essentially Lovers, rather than thinkers, full of love-consciousness which Jung took to be women's principle. Now women may emerge as worthy of emulation, not simply in their accomplishments in male domains but in their very beings.

God is not the property of religion alone but laces the whole of reality and is part of all disciplines in their search for meaning and truth.

Finally, I want to suggest two Ideas which may lead to a whole new basis for civilization than the mechanical one we have built, thanks to the seventeenth century.

One, the universe, as religions have always claimed, originates in a Lover and is like us in that it functions purposefully by intent and creative play rather than "blind." It is user-friendly, formed in love to be hospitable to every creature that inhabits it, including ourselves.

The universe likes us; it wants us here, though at present for reasons known only to itself. No doubt we have some cosmic purpose. Let barriers go down between us, the universe is a friendly place to be, we need to *commune* with it not simply form theories about it. We need to *be* with it.

Two, a proposal: Let our barriers with the Earth go down. She is not some alien being we have to make war on; these are our first cousins here. By an odd set of premises—"man alone is made in the image of God," and "have dominion over the Earth and subdue it"—taken together with technology, we have clear-cut the forests and vacuum-swept the seas. It is time to stop. We have better things to do.

We belong, not "over," not "lording it over" the others, but within and among the rest, as woman was said to be created from Adam's rib to be not above him from his head, nor beneath his feet, but at his side, to help. That is where we need to be with the animals—with them, among them, not against them. (Everybody has the sense that genetically-engineered food is not good. The molecular makeup is fine. But such foods are confused in their conscious sides about their identity, since something has been introduced to them from without, and they will only confuse us about our identities, something that none of us needs at this major turning point in history.)

We become like the gods we worship.

We have been collectively worshipping the god of mechanics for the past three hundred years, have fabricated a technology which ravages the Earth, are trying to make ourselves over into the image of our machines, as like our machines as possible in the workplace.

It is time to found a civilization based on vital, intelligent, creative play, a vibrant civilization in balance with the limits of a small living planet where the GNP includes the happiness of inhabitants. Descartes commented that in his time poetry as a way of knowing was disappearing. Now, perhaps poets may return as a way of knowing, and singing and dancing be part of the school curriculum. This new theory of the universe suggests a whole new set of values for living on this planet.

Let our economists meet the challenge of designing economies, not just for us and then only to benefit some of us, but for all the animals and plants as well, that all may have their basic needs, and then some, met.

Two popular New Age teachings may find room for themselves in this new view of the universe.

A universe of consciousness can respond to our consciousness.

First, we can use intent and prayer to modify the universe of consciousness and bring us our desires, as Jesus taught: Pray, believing that you have what you ask for, and it will be granted to you. It is our *intent* which sets in motion the physical activity of meeting a friend in a restaurant. So, clarify your intent in greater matters—e.g., having a complex situation work out in a certain way. State this to the universe and the universe of consciousness will get behind you to help you realize it. That is the nature of consciousness; it likes to be focused.

Then similarly, what you focus on, you get. Worry is a powerful prayer for what you do not want. Focus your attention on what you want, and you will put the universe into motion to help you.

Second, another proposal: I invite you to consider the possibility that reincarnation is the way the universe works, as all the oldest religions of the world attest. (Reincarnation, according to the Gnostic *Gospels,* was one of the original teachings of Jesus; it was banned by Catholicism in the fourth century and has not been taught in the West.) This is an appropriate way for a universe which is evolving, which takes time for its out-working, and whose principle is Love, for in reincarnation, justice prevails, and what you give you get in this or another lifetime. *Reincarnation is the true basis of ethics*: "Do unto others what you would have them do unto you" because whatever you give to others is going to come back to you, in this or another life. What is this to say? It says that consciousness precedes matter, we don bodies and lay them down again, hundreds of times, until (goes the teaching) our cycle of Earthly incarnations is complete, at which time we go to another destination, somewhere else in the vastness of spiritual and material worlds.

The independent *evidence* for reincarnation—past lives recalled under hypnosis—is evidence for our theory also, since reincarnation is not possible on a purely physical account.

What does this mean? Two things:

First, we came down from Heaven to be on Earth; we need to live as though we were going to stay here. We shall all end up back in the spirit world again after our Earth-life. It is time to reverse the direction of our gaze, to know that we have come down from Heaven to be on Earth and to direct all our spiritualities to really incarnating us with Love and Joy and Wisdom onto the planet.

Second, we are all immortal. We shall all meet again back in the spiritual world, even those who think the universe is nothing more than matter in motion.

The animals and plants, being essentially consciousness, reincarnate as we do, something which might pose problems for evolution, as many species have an increased ability over us to relate to the vertical, spiritual order and not simply the horizontal line of evolution. It looks as if all of us spend more time in the spiritual world than on Earth. Where do particles go when they disappear from physical reality? Back into the sea of consciousness.

Where was that patient hovering near the ceiling going after his cardiac arrest? Back into the spiritual world.

And who are we, we little race of men, women and children, and what are our ultimate purposes here on *earth*?

Ah, the question deepens, meaningful for the first time, I say: Let go of the fear associated with the separated state of the physical and a mechanical world-view and move into the Love and connectedness which is this whole, true, deep source and foundation of things and bring the ways of spirit here.

There are important implications of our theory for philosophers—a whole new way of understanding human beings. We are not individual atoms within brains and bodies, essentially separate from each other. Rather, we are all portions of God's consciousness modified by ideas and emotions. We each have an individuated consciousness, but consciousness knows no real boundaries, unlike matter; we are all essentially interconnected, deeply One, and one with our planet and her inhabitants. This is an important new understanding if we are to become one world. It is why Sages say that one cannot be happy until all are happy. Materialism focuses on our physical nature and on our differences while open-ended consciousness gives us a new openness to each other.

The view that the universe is essentially consciousness implies new ways of knowing and may affect ethics and political theory. "Having a theory about" separates us from Being, as Heidegger maintained. Abraham knew Sarah. Knowing is something like that, a communion, a oneness with what is. Truly, in a world which is essentially consciousness, knowing and being are one.

And what about the scientists? The implications for the life sciences and scientific experiment must wait until this whole new way of looking at things can be assimilated.

We can at least say our theory implies a different understanding of animals. The animals and plants have consciousness, if we attune to them. They will teach us the Beauty of the Earth we no longer know how to feel. Try experiencing the pond through the singing of the frogs on a spring night. Pure magic!

This theory implies a new approach to treating disease as, modern medicine already knows.

The theory requires a rethinking of explanation. What are the forces? All energy has consciousness. One author has called the forces "the mind of nature." (Deepak Chopra)

And this theory means that science has a new question, a new frontier: How does consciousness form matter?

Finally, the consciousness universe is the "condition of the possibility" of that mysterious Order of synchronicity—of consciousness, matter and mechanism, creative play and magic—we all experience in our lives from time to time, the openness of our souls and lives to the greater Life which allows the *I Ching* and the *Runes*, the Angel cards, to be a source of guidance for our lives.

Those are the consequences of taking "by Art" and the new principles of consciousness to be the correct account of the universe and the new emerging world-view. Physics is almost there, the life sciences need to follow.

Now, before I leave my thoughts to go forth to be with this brilliant morning, I would end by speaking of dreams.

5.

Dreams

The rest is Joy.

How can we *not* live with a sense of joy and admiration at what the universe is? This is an intelligent universe. It is always speaking to us. So St. Augustine heard children saying in a garden what seemed to be "take and read, take and read." He interpreted this as a message to read *Scripture*, he opened *Scripture* randomly, and what he read changed his life forever.

The universe speaks to us, to each one of us.

How does it speak?

It speaks symbolically, as dreams do. The first book I ever read on dreams, by John Sanford, was DREAMS: GOD'S FORGOTTEN LANGUAGE.

God speaks through dreams in *Scripture*. The whole *Book of Daniel* is a treatise on dream interpretation. Joseph is guided by dreams.

Everyone, then, valued knowing how to interpret their dreams because they were a source of guidance.

When you take your dreams seriously, they will take you seriously.

For "chance and necessity," for materialism, dreams are just the workings of the machinery.

Now we can give dreams the status they deserve. Some are more important than others, some are indeed the clear guidance of God; one can always tell them by the kind of clarity they have. I guide my life by them. Jung has given us back our rich inheritance of symbols. Now, apply them to the Day. The Day is the place where we go to meet the universe.

When anything catches your attention in the flow of life's events, ask—in love and trust, not in fear—what it means to you symbolically, and you will know what the universe is saying to you about yourself at that moment.

We live in an interactive universe, and it speaks to us.

I love going forth in the day to greet the universe, interacting with us here in the city streets as in the stars, for we are part of it and it is part of us.

At night, we turn our attention away from the physical, leave our bodies behind, and romp off back into the spiritual world to meet old friends and share stories (Jane Roberts, SETH SPEAKS).[12] In the morning, sometimes we can remember these encounters, sometimes it is just a dream. The universe is magical.

Now, a precept: Let the dream suffice. Be guided by it. Live in love and trust and connectedness rather than in the fear and separation so prevalent on Earth these past centuries. And share. How can anyone in North America be happy knowing that they are taking far more of the world's resources than is their right and that their wasteful way of life destroys, of necessity, animals and plants and human life elsewhere.

Why do philosophers write so little about love? They think much more often about grim duty than great love.

And so, I go forth to be with this lovely Christmas season in my little town of Sydney by the Sea. "By Art," in consciousness, is a cosmos fit for all and adequate to the richness of creation, an appropriate principle for a new millennium. Now I would go to be with the Day.

Stephen Pinker has written a brave book, even though it is wrong. Do not despair of answering the deep questions; we are not simply a sense-bound brain in a box. We are the Infinite Consciousness of Spirit in a body. We are fragments of God. Consciousness is open-ended, and we can know anything, though not by the methods of empirical science or mechanical models. The universe is a divine Mystery and we must enter the mystery without categories to know it by experience (the French word for "experiment").

Stephen, I urge you to go on being the bold explorer of uncharted frontiers and may the force be with you!

The universe is not merely "mechanics," though that plays a role. It is, rather, a Divine Mystery which has emerged through loving, creative play.

I exult in the Beauty and Mystery of the Universe and honour all caught up in the great drama of trying to fathom it.

All, now and then, catch a glimpse of the Forms.

Look, it goes on, the dance!

I would rather do anything than write.

All that really matters in this wonderful universe, this magical universe of ours, is Love.

Philosophers are always trying to axiomatize philosophy. How would they axiomatize the God of surprise?

What I have given here is woman's knowledge of the cosmos, the "condition of the possibility" of being fully alive here in the Earth plane, something I learned in a wilderness life.

It is also the germ of a systematic Metaphysics—in so far as the God of surprise permits Itself to be systematized—a systematic metaphysics written in both masculine and feminine modes.

It is also, I dare say, what a Feminine Plato would have to say, here at a new Beginning for us, the dawn of the third millennium.

The new frontiers: Interacting with spiritual beings; bringing Spirit here.

A new empiricism.

*   *   *

I have arrived at this view of the universe through discussions with a non-physical entity, Voice of Light, channelled through a friend, Cherionna Menzam.

With grateful thanks to Don Knight who made me aware of Pinker's book and to Angela Wall for fine tuning.

A shortened version of these two essays, "Beyond Chance and Necessity" and "A New Theory of the Universe," appears in the *Journal of Speculative Philosophy*, 2003

6.

References

[1] Pert, C., MOLECULES OF EMOTION, Simon and Shuster NY 1999.

[2] Plato, THE REPUBLIC, COMPLETE WORKS, Cooper, E. and D. Hutchinson, (eds.) Hacket Pub. Co. IN 1997.

[3] Penrose, R., THE EMPEROR'S NEW MIND, Penguin NY 1991.

[4] Talbot, M., THE HOLOGRAPHIC UNIVERSE, Harper Pub. Perennial Library CA 1992.

[5] Bohm, D., WHOLENESS AND THE IMPLICATE ORDER, Routledge KY 1996.

[6] Zohar, D., THE QUANTUM SELF, Quill TX 1991.

[7] Goswami, A., THE SELF-AWARE UNIVERSE: HOW CONSCIOUS-NESS FORMS MATTER, J.P. Tacher NY 1995.

[8] Davies, P. and J. Gribbins, THE MATTER MYTH, Simon and Schuster NY 1992.

[9] Penrose, R., SHADOWS OF THE MIND, Oxford University Press UK 1996.

[10] Crick, F., THE ASTONISHING HYPOTHESIS: SCIENTIFIC SEARCH FOR THE SOUL, Touchstone Books OR 1995.

[11] Edelman, G. and G. Tononi, A UNIVERSE OF CONSCIOUSNESS: HOW MATTER BECOMES IMAGINATION, Basic Books NY 2000.

[12] Roberts, J., SETH SPEAKS, Amber-Allen Pub. New World Library San Rafael, CA 1994.

III

The Spiritual Dimensions of Mental Illness

The Spiritual Dimensions of Mental Illness

An open letter to the psychiatric profession and to all who fear mental illness, from a former patient.

You would not find out the boundaries of soul by travelling in any direction, so deep a measure does it have.

—Heraclitus, 500 B.C.

Table of Contents—Essay III

Introduction

As a clinical psychologist trained within the framework of the "scientist-practitioner" model, I am generally comfortable with the methods of empirical science and the formal classification systems that have been advanced to organize and guide our understanding of the human condition. Within the routine of a clinical setting, the classification systems and explanatory theoretical models provide safe haven and consequently are seldom challenged. Although there is general agreement with regard to their heuristic value, their philosophical and metaphysical underpinnings are rarely considered. Despite these obvious contributions of scientific inquiry to current advances in the cognitive sciences as well as the diagnosis, classification and treatment of a myriad of mental conditions, one must obviously be cautioned against accepting so narrow a view of human experience as representative of some fundamental truth. Ultimately, there are limits to the scientific understanding of man.

Kant argued that positivism, the principle tenet of which holds that experience is the sole source of knowledge and thus the methods of empirical science the only means by which the world could be understood, derived from an inadequate understanding of the mind, and held that the mind constructed reality from experience by using innate concepts. Thus to understand man, Kant felt it necessary to try to fathom the nature of his deep and universal cognitive endowment. Sensory impressions became experience, that is, gained meaning, only after they were interpreted in terms of *a priori* concepts, such as time, space and causality. Kant referred to these concepts as "transcendental" because they transcended experience and, consequently were considered beyond the scope of scientific inquiry.

My first encounter with Lorna was as a consulting psychologist in the in-patient unit where she was hospitalized during the summer of 1983. Although the ostensible reason for the referral was to provide consultation regarding the diagnosis, there was also much interest around the fact that this "woman of science" had had a psychotic episode—a "break from reality." Somehow, this apparent inconsistency challenged the conventional view that reason should prevail over madness. What was most interesting, in retrospect, was that the staff were far more distressed by this apparent inconsistency than Lorna herself! She described a blissful state filled with personal meaning and fully understood within the context of her spiritual life. We discussed at length the phenomenological aspects of her experience and left behind the relatively inconsequential matter of diagnosis. Thus began a relationship that has continued over the past fifteen years and has provided frequent opportunity for thought and reflection. Over the years Lorna has visited me either in person or with the gift of her writing. I am richer for it and would hope that others might reflect and be challenged as I have been to consider the broader context and meaning of their experience

John Gainer, Ph.D.
Sydney, NS, Canada
September, 1998

The Spiritual Dimensions of Mental Illness

An Open Letter to the Psychiatric Profession and to All Who Fear Mental Illness, from a Former Patient

I am privileged to have been hospitalized three times in mental institutions. First, I was in the Payne-Whitney Clinic in New York City, in 1966, for five months. Then, on returning to my homeland, Canada, in 1979, I was in the Nova Scotia Hospital, Halifax, for eleven days. Finally, I was in the Cape Breton Mental Health Hospital, Sydney, for approximately two weeks, in the summer of 1983.

Plato thought physicians should have the diseases they treat in order to better understand the internal state of their patients. Few of you have been hospitalized, or know the inner of the illnesses that you attempt to cure. I would like, therefore, to tell you something of this inner side, and its implications for treatment, in order that much suffering might be prevented in future for other patients. In particular, I want to speak to you of the spiritual dimensions. One really cannot treat the emotional and the physical while neglecting the spiritual. All my hospitalizations had strong religious overtones, especially the more recent ones. I would speak to you in particular of these religious aspects.

The Aesculapian tradition of Greek medicine held that one had to be ill to know the gods. All illness is redemptive and belongs as much to our life with God as our life in the world. This may be especially true of those illnesses in which our behaviour appears so unusual by ordinary standards and in which one seems to lose contact with the ordinary world. You may wonder what is happening on the inner side. It is a standard joke that some patients on mental wards believe they are Christ, and that truck drivers write about the soul. What is really happening in these mysterious occurrences?

I believe that "mental illness" in my case has been part of my life with God. I do not treat these Mysteries lightly. Before doing so, let me set before you my qualifications.

I received a BSc from McGill University, Montreal, in 1960. I subsequently did graduate work at The Rockefeller University in New York City and graduated with a PhD in the life sciences in 1965. I received an MA in philosophy from the University of Toronto in 1970, and while finishing a doctoral dissertation in philosophy (which I never defended), taught the great books at St. Johns College in Santa Fe, New Mexico.

In 1975 I discovered the Benedictine Monastery of Pecos, New Mexico, and spent several periods during the following years deepening into the truths they had to teach. Pecos is charismatic and teaches much Jungian depth psychology. From Abbot David I learned a great deal about the ways of a Catholic and have been following a path of prayer and writing ever since.

I have published two books: The first, my thesis in philosophy, THE VERIFICATION OF METAPHYSICAL THEORIES: ETHICS AS BASIS FOR METAPHYSICS with Interface Press in 1985; the second, EARTH AGE: A NEW VISION OF GOD, THE HUMAN AND THE EARTH, with Paulist Press in 1994. Two more, THE REIGN OF THE HOLY SPIRIT (1996) and GUIDING PRINCIPLES FOR THE PLANET (1998) are currently being read by publishers. A fifth work, THE FEMININE, is in process.

1.

The Payne-Whitney Clinic, New York, 1966

I was hospitalized in the Payne-Whitney Clinic, New York City Hospital, in January, 1966. I had just defended a difficult PhD thesis in science that fall, and a beloved philosophy teacher, Ludwig Edelstein, had died suddenly in August, the first death of someone close to me. I had begun to read, alone, Kant's THE CRITIQUE OF PURE REASON (when Kant had finished writing this work, he gave it to a friend to read, but the friend soon handed it back, saying: "I dare not read further, or I shall lose my sanity"). Otherwise, I could not make up my mind as to just what I should be doing. My friend, Don Knight, who had studied with Edelstein also, was at Harvard while I was in New York. I was torn between wanting to stay in New York and continue the studies I had planned with Edelstein and wanting to go to Cambridge to be with Don. I also felt a great desire to marry him, a desire new to me who had always wished to remain single. I was also trying to find my way back to God and to embark on a contemplative life.

In addition, I had gone home to Toronto for Christmas holidays and expressed a ton of anger at my father, whom I accused of never seeing me as I was but only viewed me as someone who did science.

So one night in January, 1966, with my passions for Don suppressed for so long (while writing the thesis) cascading around me and with some most terrifying memories and fears from childhood flooding up, I walked into the nearby Payne-Whitney Mental Clinic and signed myself in.

Moments of that night are noteworthy. When I entered the front vestibule, I prostrated myself on the ground in the form of a cross. The night attendant urged me to get up. Little could he know that I was identifying myself with a film I had seen in which a young nun left her convent and her vows in order to live with various lovers, all of whom were killed. She suddenly realized the pattern, and returned to the convent and prostrated herself before the altar. As she did so, a statue of the Blessed Virgin which had stepped down when she left, stepped back into place. Given my recent past behaviour, my act was quite rational. At some level of my being, I knew I had offended God and must return to Him.

I was given a room on the seventh floor, the admitting ward. There, especially in my mind, was an image the philosopher Descartes had in one of his youthful dreams, a *sic et non*, yes and no. He had interpreted his dream as a need for higher synthesis. In all subsequent hospitalizations I have seen this image. I, too, have always interpreted this to mean that higher synthesis was occurring.

I saw a woman doctor, and believing that one must tell psychiatrists all that is in one's depths, I spilled out of all kinds of ideas. She told me that my unconscious was coming up "too fast." This remark frightened me and made me very apprehensive.

I was subsequently placed in a locked ward with a great many depressed older women. I had never in my life before been with older women, let alone depressed ones. I was told I must learn to make small talk, that I had been too intellectual and that my philosophical interests were a mistake. When in anguish I told the doctor about Kant, she told me that all those things would fall into place when I was well again, and that they were just "ideas." (On the contrary, my whole system of reality had been turned upside down by them.) I was also told, on the basis of my behaviour, that my mother had a weak ego and that I must now begin to examine, in the presence of the doctors, what things meant to me. For example, what was it about the colour brown of my dress that fascinated me? My thought was only of the dress's simplicity of line. Being a deeply private person, I was disinclined to share my private feelings under a cold clinical light. I was also told that writing in notebooks, which was where I thought out the whole of science for myself and discovered that it rested in "unexplained explainers," showed an absence of relationship and that I was using writing as a refuge.

In my weakened condition, I was told many other things about myself which would have been far better left unsaid. These have haunted me for years. I had been a strong, robust person, bicycling freely about the streets of New York. To take such a one and put her behind locked doors boded only trouble. In no time I developed free-floating anxiety. I could not bear to be within the hospital, but I could not bear to be outside it either. I was not comfortable anywhere. I was afraid of elevators, enclosed spaces, heights, traffic, other people.

If you have never experienced free-floating anxiety, you cannot imagine how devastating it is. This was to persist in me about ten years, rendering me unable to go anywhere by myself. It did not disappear until I came to the monastery in New Mexico and encountered the Divine Healer.

My hospital stay was mitigated by the fact that Don came to visit almost every day (until they even disallowed that), and that I had a woman doctor, who was a mother and who would patiently listen to my complaints about the anxiety and to my requests to be taken into her home or given physical work to do.

I came into the hospital experiencing tremendous guilt for the first time in my life. This happened again while I was in Toronto. I was told, on both occasions, that guilt was an unhealthy way of thinking and would go away when I was better. (It was only many years later that I would learn, at a monastery, that guilt is real because we all too often transgress against the divine inner image of the self God made. At the monastery, I would discover that I could bring my guilt before God and repent of it and be restored to my real self. A nun told me that one is most oneself after repentance. I am never far from a little book written by another nun, called REPENTANCE, THE JOY-FILLED LIFE. Since that time I have made frequent use of the great cleansing power of the sacrament of reconciliation, as it is called in the church, and would recommend it to all).

When I asked how long I must stay in hospital, I was put off with indefinite replies. Every time I broached the possibility of signing myself out, the subject was dropped. I had not enough self-confidence, stripped as I was of almost all aspects of my identity, to insist. Finally, they told me that in an "illness" of my sort, the recovery time was five to six months. They kept me there about five months, by an amazing coincidence, just the time until the private insurance monies ran out.

The Payne-Whitney was wrong about guilt, about my mother, about locked doors, and about my lack of relationships—I had many friends, as friends were in those days, with whom I had shared the camaraderie of science. It was also wrong about long stays.

My doctor also told me I would always have to have a "structured day." As it is, I detest the structured day, and, at fifty-nine, live with loose self-structure according to my flow of energies and "the singing heart."

The Payne-Whitney was wrong about medication. I was on 1600 mgs. of Mellaril a day to which I developed pigment deposition in the retina, a side-effect not discovered in my case until four years later because it was initially missed by an intern who failed to dilate my retina before making his examination. Today, I am losing my eyesight because of the pigmentation.

Many serious negative consequences flowed from this hospitalization *which could have been avoided.* I experienced a severe loss of my sense of my own identity. I no longer had any sense of the continuity of life but felt torn out of context. I had no idea what had happened to me. They told me I had a schizoid break. At the monastery I heard for the first time of the inruption of the unconscious and the healing power it confers. The most I was told at the Payne-Whitney was that this happened to many other people, and they recovered. I have to admit, this was some consolation. But I have always needed to understand what was happening to me in order to accept it. I had no understanding at all from my doctors. I was also taught to totally distrust my love of philosophy since it was a "flight from reality" and to get in touch with the "real world."

This hospitalization left a sensitive and strong-willed girl with deep scars which it has taken many, many years of living to heal.

I have puzzled about this hospitalization a great deal. Only when I was at the monastery in Pecos did I begin to be at rest about the experience, for there I came to see it as God sees it. The Abbot said one day in a lecture: "The way down is the way up, even in the most expensive hospital in New York." The Payne-Whitney *is* the most expensive hospital in New York. A beautiful nun told me: "You had to know your poverty." And I understood then that my arrogant spirit had to be humbled. I went from proud independence in New York to total dependence on Don. I was like a child, and have remained so, in many ways, until this day. (Don is an extremely gentle person, who has mothered me all these years.)

Later, at Pecos, I remembered one night in the Payne-Whitney when I stood at my window, looking out on the rainy streets below, and felt the presence of God. I knew, then at the monastery, that He had been with me even in the hospital, that it was part of His will for me. "The Lord chasteneth those whom He loveth." Ten years later, I could accept it as part of the story of my life, in some higher perspective. Yet it was also the worst, most painful and most humiliating experience of my life.

Looking back, I see that I was young enough and resilient enough to take it.

All happens within the Divine Will. In the summer of 1984, realizing how much my spirit had needed tempering, I found myself thanking God for the experience of the Payne-Whitney seventeen years before. But you can guess how much deep inner healing was necessary in order to be able to say that.

2.

Toronto, 1966-72

Upon discharge from the New York Clinic, I came to Toronto, my family's home. Don came to study philosophy at the University of Toronto Graduate School. I had nowhere else to go. All my thoughts of love and marriage had vanished. I was too inwardly dislocated and disarrayed for anything like that.

I did not take up the study of philosophy as I had planned to in New York, for everyone around me distrusted my interest in it. Instead, I worked at part-time jobs in bookstores and finally, to do something familiar, I took a medical research position at the Wellesley Hospital. Friends and family were pleased for, after all, my training had been in science.

I made the best of it, attending seminars and lectures, and doing research in the lab. But in four months, I knew the truth, and no one would ever again shake me from it: I was finished with science forever. I no longer belonged there. (While at the Rockefeller University, I had come to the conclusion that science could not explain the world, and there was, therefore, no further reason for me to do it.)

But where to turn?

I was filled with anxiety all this time and seldom dared to speak to anyone. Then, one night, I saw a seminar advertised near the university on "Freedom and Determinism." I had thought a great deal about these subjects at Rockefeller and decided to go along and listen. To my surprise, part of the way through the discussion, I heard myself speaking in an incisive and clear way, putting the discussion to rights. Everyone listened. Afterwards, when the discussion resumed, I was so amazed at what I had done, anxieties surged up and I left the gathering and came home.

But, once again, I had *experienced* where I belonged. My way was clear. I knew I wanted to spend my life engaged in such discussions.

I told Don of my triumph and desire. A few days later, there mysteriously appeared on my desk application forms for the University of Toronto.

At that time I was seeing a psychiatrist at the Toronto General Hospital, Dr. George Renecker. I had no in-depth therapy, but met to discuss how I was coping. He was a young man, about my age. We had "reality therapy." I kept my decision to study philosophy secret from both family and Dr. Renecker, knowing the attitudes of both to the study of philosophy and also knowing their power, in my precarious state, to deflect my will.

As the time neared for entry, I knew Dr. Renecker must be told. So at the end of one of our sessions, I said: "By the way, I am going to study philosophy, beginning next week."

He never hid from me his emotions. His jaw dropped, but there was no time for comment as it was the end of a session. By the following week, his initial reaction to my announcement had been carefully camouflaged.

My family opposed the decision, but I did not care. I knew with certainty what I wanted. For the subsequent year, the fact that I was studying philosophy was completely ignored when I visited them in their house. (I did not live with them in the suburbs, but downtown).

That year was a lesson for all. Within four months of studying philosophy, anxieties were minimal, my mind was functioning again and I was back in shape. I felt like a person, I could talk to people, and I could work.

Dr. Renecker was amazed at the effects of my philosophical studies. Philosophy is, in fact, an excellent treatment for people like me who have been hospitalized, because it is thinking about reality, a function which falls into disrepair in so-called "mental illness." A friend of mine, in later years, told me she met a woman in New York reading Kant's THE CRITIQUE OF PURE REASON to put her mind back together after a nervous breakdown. Reading, thinking, and most especially conversing with other students were the activities which began to heal me. I learned the gift of others. My mind was restructured by other people.

In the beginning, I had no concentration and had to write down every question I wanted to ask. But within some weeks I could participate in the discussion as freely as anyone.

The study of philosophy reconstituted a sense of identity I had had at Rockefeller where I had raised all these questions, largely by myself. Here, everyone was thinking about scientific explanation, necessity, ethics, and freedom. I was in paradise. During the first year, I explored all the issues I had explored in New York. And then, I turned seriously to the study of philosophy, seeking for the truth of *what things were* since I no longer believed that science could explain the universe.

I flowered. I looked just like an ordinary person, except for the anxieties which were always there, and except for my deep emotional dependence on Don who continually encouraged me. He did not see me as I was, a "bundle of nerves," but remembered me as I had been, full of strength and daring. His belief in me helped me grow back into some semblance of my former self.

I studied philosophy at Toronto formally for three years, falling in and out of love several times, and began to have a life again. I was happy in Toronto and at ease in the city.

Then Don left Toronto to live in Santa Fe, New Mexico. At one time before he left, I felt the full weight of rage of my dependency on him and a tremendous anger surfaced which I did not express. Dr. Renecker told me that my anger was to "abstractions" and that I must stay in the present. In this, as I discovered years later, he was wrong. Old anger is real in us and must be expressed. I would express it finally at a monastery.

I visited Don in New Mexico. On Friday nights, St. Johns College held formal lectures with guest speakers. I went to such a lecture, and found myself holding forth in the question period afterwards. They offered me a job. I accepted and came to New Mexico to teach. My first teaching position, at age thirty-three. Dr. Renecker, who knew me well, advised me to let myself savour and enjoy it. Good advice.

My path has often been configured for me by the words of others. Before leaving for New Mexico, I talked to a friend from Colorado. He told me: "Colorado is beautiful, but New Mexico is mystical."

Mystical. That was the first time this word had crossed my life.

I went to the desert and found what those who go to deserts find.

3.

Santa Fe, N.M., 1972-1979

I lived in a small adobe house on a hill overlooking the town of Santa Fe, two blocks from the Cathedral of St. Francis. From there, I heard its bells, and while preparing my classes, delighted in fall rains, desert skies, clear air, the stars at night. Cosmos, after Toronto.

On the weekends, we hiked in the mountains. Don lived at the other side of town, and I went everywhere on a moped which gave me independence. The anxiety was there and my inner being was in disarray, but I knew now how to live with that state and to keep the anxieties minimal.

I taught for three years, while working on a doctoral thesis for the philosophy department at the University of Toronto. I thrived on contact with students and their ready friendships and on the responsibilities associated with teaching.

In my third year, exhausted by having no summer holiday and from wrestling with the thesis, I experienced a deep depression upon returning to the college in the fall. For this I received 50 mgs. per day of Tofranil. I was also on a maintenance dose of tranquillizer, Haldol, 5 mgs. per day.

I had almost finished my thesis, still seeking the truth, when I discovered, on the recommendation of a student, the Benedictine Monastery in nearby Pecos, New Mexico. Pecos was charismatic, a mixed community of men and women. I was at first afraid to go, but I also knew that I must. On my first visit, I took one look at the faces of the community members and knew, by the joy and laughter there, that they had the truth. But what was that truth? I went back many times that spring to find out, and when I did I built it into the conclusion of my thesis. After my first visit my anger at the college where I was teaching surfaced. I threw rocks each morning before math class, up in the hills behind the school. The depression vanished. That summer I resigned my teaching job and made a thirty-day retreat at the monastery. That was when my healing began in depth. I shall tell you something about it.

4.

Benedictine Monastery, NM, 1975-79

Monasteries are as concerned as the medical profession with healing. When Christ was with us, he healed the sick. He still heals. At Pecos, in the presence of the Divine physician, the healing of my inner being took place.

I was at Pecos twice for extended visits, with many in-between visits. First, I made a summer retreat of one month. During that time, a very ancient relationship to God was restored and I began to make the acquaintance of the Lord. My second stay was the subsequent winter during Lent, for two months. During this time, I was restored and healed of many hurts lying buried in the past, hurts from that childhood whose memories and fears had erupted around me the night I walked into Payne-Whitney.

The Pecos community, as I mentioned, was Benedictine and charismatic, and the men and women there lived under vows of poverty, chastity and obedience. Community life was structured around four prayer services a day—morning praise, mass, vespers and compline. The rest of the time the members worked at Dove Publications or at various tasks around the monastery.

The abbot told us: "When you come to a monastery, tell God what you want of Him and pay attention to your first dream, for in it He often tells you what He is going to do with you."

My first dream was of myself, taking off a heavy fur coat. A friend said: *"The unveiling of the woman."*

I told God I wanted to see my life and to be healed of its many hurts. In the gentle, feminine, healing atmosphere of the monastery, so different from that of academic life, I laid down my arduous quest for truth and was happy just to listen to the many wonderful teachings of Abbot David about the way God works with us—e.g., bringing us around to the same situations again and again until we turn and ask for healing. He spoke much about inner healing and about Jungian depth psychology. And we all dreamed much and learned to interpret our dreams.

Shortly after my arrival, several of us were sharing aspects of our lives with each other. As I heard a grandmother weep because her father died without receiving the sacraments, I discovered tears just streaming from my eyes and flowing down my face. That is the "gift of tears," and it is a well-known phenomenon in monasteries. It is considered a sign that God is healing the interior being. I was to experience those tears many times when there, though I thought of myself as the sort of person who never cried over anything.

I drew a little apart to be by myself and realized that I was mourning the death of my beloved professor in New York some ten years previous. I had never mourned at the time, being instead preoccupied with finishing a thesis.

I found a beautiful nun who introduced me to the mysteries of the faith and with whom I shared my feelings about how that professor had been a wonderful model for God because he wanted us to think out everything for ourselves.

That night I lay in bed unable to sleep. Suddenly I sensed that the room was filled with a mysterious and comforting presence. I knew from the Abbot's teachings that this is one of the ways God manifests himself. As I lay there in perfect security, I found myself remembering childhood, not from the outside as so many of our memories are, but from the inside—the smell of cookies on a rainy Saturday, rain streaming down the window. Then I remembered my teenage years of canoeing and the beauty of the paddle cleaving dark waters.

As I lay there, a very early memory came—of me, very small, running out in grasses with my parents, two gentle, reassuring presences behind me. The grasses were eye-high. But it was not the grasses I was seeing. It was that same presence now filling the room which I sensed. Then I knew that God had been with me from the beginning of my life; as I lay bathed in memory, I saw the many other times when He had crossed my path, even in the Payne-Whitney, though I had never had the name. Rather, I had called it "heightened sensation." I had wandered a long way from the unspoilt world of childhood.

I also saw, in this image, that my mother, whom I had thought of as having a "weak ego," was, in fact, a saint.

After that night—the first time I had remembered anything of childhood since the Payne-Whitney—and safe in the Abbot's teachings and in the gentleness and the feminine security of the monastery, I came in touch with my unconscious life. A deep, interior life now began. Especially did I get in touch with the memories of my teenage years when I had been torn from my secure context in Canada with teenage friends and loves to move to the United States at the beginning of my fourth year in high school. I saw in how many ways I had been wandering in the world since that time, always remaining in a place about five years until I would be uprooted for some other place.

All the wounds and pain of those years were opened up. In an atmosphere of prayer there was always someone to pray with. When anyone prays with you for old pain, a great peace enters the psyche and living waters flow on the inside. Aridity and inner turmoil give way to living waters and peace. For the first time since entering the hospital ten years before, I began to feel a stillness and ease within myself.

During this first visit, I spent much time alone with God—by streams, in the hills, in the prayer services of the community. I deepened into the great joy of my teenage "religious phase."

God wove me back and forth through my life, recent and early, opening up the painful spots for his healing touch. I began to peek into very early childhood and wondered if I could face it. I did not know what was there but I was afraid of it nonetheless. When at Mass I heard: "I have put aside childish things." I knew I would not necessarily have to go there. I returned to Santa Fe to deepen into my new relationship with God. Anxieties had vanished. At thirty-six, I was a free, transformed being. "Late have I loved you, oh Beauty so ancient and so new." (St. Augustine)

The next phase of my healing occurred at Catherine Dougherty's community in Combermere, Ontario. I had wanted to meet Catherine for some time. She is a charismatic Russian baroness who knows how to listen to God. I travelled north from Santa Fe, alone, to meet her. While there, I made a poustinia—a day and night of prayer and fasting in a little hermitage in the woods. I came in touch with terror, a terror so great that I left the poustinia and returned to the dormitories to try to get a grip on myself. It reminded me of the terror I experienced the night I walked into the Payne-Whitney. When I told a priest of my experience the next day, he heard the words in his mind: "Birth trauma." So he prayed for the circumstances of my birth, and I felt a greater upsurge of warmth and beauty than I had ever felt before. I returned to Toronto in a state of peace and joy. Again, alone. For the first time in ten years, I was willing and able to be by myself.

I speak of healing prayer. The charismatic movement in the church has recovered the powers of healing possessed by the early church. Physical healings are common, and I witnessed many of them at Pecos. But even more wonderful are the ministries of "inner healing." Ways are being found to pray for the pains of our life which lie buried in the past. Freud discovered such pain but could do little for it beyond making it conscious. Now, these pains can be prayed for, with inner images of Christ, or with other healing images. One can feel the effects in one's psyche when prayed for. God is not just the most wonderful subject to think about but is also the most wonderful to feel. Healing waters and interior life are real, well-known to the religious tradition.

Religious communities are places in which the depths of one's inner being come up. For one is the Divine icon, and all that is not of God surfaces to be dealt with or healed. One's entire past is re-worked as the true self appears.

When I came to the monastery for the first time, I was still full of anxiety. I only knew that they had something wonderful there and that I wanted it. After that experience, I was no longer dependent on Don but on the Lord. I had learned the Jesus prayer at the monastery: "Jesus, Lord Jesus," co-ordinated with the breathing. The Abbot had reported teaching this prayer to the inmates of mental hospitals and of seeing them leave reciting it. Its effects are almost immediate—an interior warming, a peace. I rode trains, buses and planes to go to Combermere by myself on the simple and sure strength of that prayer.

My second stay in Pecos was the winter after returning from Combermere. In all my new enthusiasm, I experienced a loss of identity seeing people and parents in Canada. By the time I returned to Santa Fe, I felt deeply depressed. I had lost God and was in no way certain of what I should be doing. The Abbot invited me to come to Pecos with an eye to joining the community permanently. I went, depressed and fearful.

Again, the first dream was important. I dreamed that I had gone to hear Jesus give a talk with a young male friend my own age. After the talk, I asked Jesus questions and he said to me in a friendly, laughing, knowing way: "Let us go visit that old man who is lying in hospital with his stomach opened." He looked older, yet younger than me. I wondered how we would get there. Would we fly?

A few days later, I realized that this man was my father as he had looked to me when I was a young child. The Abbot confirmed this: "God is going to work with your father image."

I take it there is no need to say anything to the psychiatric profession about what father and mother images are. As the Abbot put it: "Our father image, because of our traditions, shapes what we will think of God and how we will relate to him, to men around us, and to authority."

Again, vivid dreams marked what was happening in my inner life. The depths yielded memories. I came in touch with tremendous fears which I had had of my father as a young child, fears and fascination, and a sense of rejection, this latter probably because I was a Spock baby and was never picked up when I cried. There were the fears I had of moving to a new house and memories of sibling rivalries. I had vivid memories that I was always striving to be appreciated by my father and that all he valued was school-work. I felt that I was not loved for myself. Tremendous anger for all sorts of memories of slights and injustices surfaced. I expressed them by throwing rocks in the hills. I also came in touch with my love of school and of learning.

I was beginning to learn to handle these depths in images. I developed a very close relationship with the Lord by praying in powerful images with a friend each night. How much pain was prayed through!

I did not dare to think of God. When you are afraid of your father, you are very afraid of God. I clung to Jesus, my brother, and to the anchorage of real people in the community.

Everything that happened to me had to do with healing of my father image and with my relationships from it with other men. Getting in touch with my own femininity and developing a sense of my validity as a woman also became very important. As one of the nuns put it: "Your outer being can range in philosophy. Now God is catching up your inner being."

I joined the Catholic Church at Pecos on Easter Eve, 1977. At Pecos I had seen and experienced what can almost never be seen in the world—the warm, living heart of the Church. I strongly recommend a visit there for learning the nature of spiritual reality. *Everyone* could feel the presence of the Lord at services.

At the very end of my stay, the day before I was to go home (God is completely reliable), I had a dream about my standing by, witnessing my father's life. I saw all his interests, his flying days. At one point, he turned and invited me into the dream and took me home with him to meet his family. They were a quarrelsome lot, and I understood completely why my father bolted down his supper and ran outside to look at the stars.

I realized, in a way words could never tell, just how different my father's life was from mine, what different people we were. No one had ever encouraged him in his studies—I took his encouragement as pressure. No one had believed in him when he was young, and all his life he had striven to please the father he could never please, even as I had striven to please him. I understood that for him science represented freedom where for me it represented knowledge. I came away from that dream with a deep understanding and sense of reconciliation with my father which has persisted, with some ups and downs and new bursts of healing, to this day. The old father image is still there, but increasingly as I recognize it and know it, it functions less as a determinant of my life.

Another interesting consequence flowed. I had always fallen in love with either older men or younger students, never with people my own age. Now, God began bringing me to people my own age, and I found myself loving them as much as the others. For the first time, Don functioned less as a mother and more as someone I might marry. A great deal of inner work flowed from those two sessions at the monastery.

I came out to live and work at odd jobs in Santa Fe for several years, deepening into a life of prayer and writing. I had a dream about St. Teresa of Avila, so I followed the Carmelite way of prayer laid down by her along with that of St. John of the Cross. I learned a great deal about prayer and about the religious life. I made the acquaintance of Mother

Rose Teresa, the superior of the Carmelites, a completely cloistered order whose members spend their whole lives in prayer. How I yearned to join that order and partake in its peace and depths of Realness. But I gradually came to see that I must find its peace outside the cloister.

As I deepened into a life of prayer, it became clear to me that my life in Santa Fe was over. Don was still a good friend. I was increasingly independent of him. But where to go? I had visited Nova Scotia and loved it. I would like to go there. But where did God want me? I had learned a great deal about asking this question and answering it from studies with Abbot David.

By this time I had written a series of essays entitled: WHERE PHI-LOSOPHY MEETS GOD: AN ESSAY ON IDENTITY (The Underpinnings of the Silent Life—Towards the Feminine Principle). I had also learned to pray in the Ignatian way, over *Scripture*. This way of prayer was worked out by St. Ignatius Loyola, the founder of the Jesuit Order. One makes a solitary retreat and is given passages of scripture by a director. As one reads and responds to what one is given, the guide senses the direction in which the Spirit is leading and gives new passages. In this way, one is led deeper and deeper into experiences of God in prayer and into the depths of oneself.

I decided to make such a retreat and to learn of God what he wanted me to do and where he wanted me to do it. I was forty years old. As I entered the mountain property of the retreat centre, a site of orchards and streams, I heard an inner voice say: "This is Nova Scotia." All my dreams were of Nova Scotia. Guided by the retreat director, I was led into deep and wonderful experiences which bear telling in some other place.

I was told to go to Nova Scotia and start a house of prayer.

5.

Interlude: The Spiritual Traditions

Before I describe the spiritual dimensions of two subsequent hospitalizations, I want to speak of the spiritual tradition of the church and of its significance for modern psychiatry. For a great deal is known there about interior life and inner healing.

Christianity today has a bad name both as the tyrant of Western thought, beliefs, and doctrines and as dead churches without real spiritualism. What many do not realize is that there is a rich mystical tradition of Christian thought and practice being recovered in our time.

St. John of the Cross in his THE DARK NIGHT OF THE SOUL and his LIVING FLAME OF LOVE and St. Teresa of Avila in her THE INTERIOR CASTLE are both adept at describing inner life and the progress through periods of exaltation and aridity of that life towards a state they call "union with God." No one is as clear at describing these states as St. Teresa. She claims that God himself dwells in the centre of our soul, and as we leave off our preoccupations with outer events and withdraw inwardly, we contact him. (Psychological phenomena resembling psychotic episodes are not uncommon in a life of prayer).

The Catholic tradition maintains that the Holy Trinity dwells in the depths of our beings. It would be surprising if, from time to time, we did not slip into it.

I have mentioned the charismatic movement of the church. This movement has recovered the powers of the Holy Spirit. Once again what Jesus told the disciples of John the Baptist who inquired if he were the Messiah is true: "The blind see, the lame walk, the poor have the good news preached to them." The Holy Spirit seems to want health and healing for us just as Christ wanted it when he was among us.

The Spirit also mediates a close experiential relationship with Christ. He is not someone who merely lived two thousand years ago and left a body of teachings. Nor is he a mere idea. He is a real being of the spiritual world and will come to us in the depths of prayer. The Jesus prayer is a privileged way of contacting him since he comes in response to his name.

The healing experienced at monasteries (I have visited many) is well-known within the church. It is entirely spirit-guided and the Spirit never sends one more than can be handled. When working with this power, the influx from the depths is relatively smooth and orderly. The inner is evoked by circumstances of the outer. In the atmosphere of deep love and acceptance, the wounds of the inner being are opened to be healed.

At Pecos I learned something of Jungian depth psychology. I learned that there is a narrow boundary between the conscious and the unconscious life which is occasionally crossed by an inruption from the unconscious. The spiritual tradition recognizes that this inruption or wounding of the conscious self confers upon that self great power of healing. The shamans of Native American tribes were those wounded by such inruptions. The way down is the way up even in the most expensive hospital in New York.

Jung's theories are perhaps the most detailed we have on the nature of the psyche. But just how deep are we? Abbot David taught that the entrance to the whole spiritual world is within us. Perhaps the psychiatric profession knows this already.

Jung said that what he knew about the soul derived from Catholic spiritual direction during a particularly auspicious time in the life of the church.

6.

Nova Scotia Hospital, Dartmouth, 1979

My second hospitalization was thirteen years after that of the Payne-Whitney. It was a wonderful and amazing experience. I would not have missed it for anything, though it only lasted eleven days.

I came to Nova Scotia seeking a suitable place for a house of prayer. First I was with the Sisters of St. Martha and then with some contemplative nuns building hermitages for themselves on Cape Breton Island. I experienced considerable culture shock coming from Santa Fe to Nova Scotia. Despite my strong faith and knowledge of how to detect the leadings of God, anxiety about where to settle appeared. I wanted only to be somewhere living quietly with God, but instead, became quite worn out with all the impressions of travel. I finally came to a place which seemed right and decided to make a solitary retreat with God and replenish my energies.

There was a retreat house nearby. The director was away, but I was admitted and began to organize my own solitary retreat over scriptural passages. I felt, from the difficulties of getting to this place, that I had in some way damaged my inner being, and I was experiencing manic states early in my retreat. That is almost all I remember. A day or two escapes me. My last memory of the retreat is of the director entering my room while I was in deep prayer. (This interruption is something one should never do). Afterwards I apparently acted strangely at dinner and was taken to the local hospital where I vented a tremendous anger on the doctors. I remember none of this, however. When I "came to myself," as it is sometimes put, I was in the Nova Scotia Hospital, in Dartmouth.

From the very beginning my stay was rich in the mysteries of spiritual life. I arrived on the ward and felt at once that I was in a place (though I did not know it was a hospital) which would integrate my entire life. The people of all ages (most wore ordinary dress), the views of the sea outside, the autumn light, even the graffiti on the walls, reminded me of places I had been. I had always valued integration. I looked around me with compassion and awe, and an older woman standing beside me said but one word: "Pray."

Pray. From a patient on a hospital ward?

My second experience of the mysterious came while I was in the woman's washroom being helped into a johnny shirt. I looked at myself in the mirror with my hair hanging over my face—my bobby pins had been confiscated—and I thought to myself, inwardly: "Am I mad"? The same woman was standing beside me and said: "No." I was later put into a room with her and two others.

I saw a doctor only briefly on admission. I was there for eleven days and did not see another doctor again until I was to be discharged. I shall always be grateful to the doctors that they left us alone. I do not know if this was deliberate policy on their part, but, if so, it was very enlightened. Patients ministered to each other out of the knowledge and care that we were all deep in spiritual experience.

At the beginning, I was so deeply within myself that I had lost language. I had the feeling of standing deep within swirling waters. When one cannot say anything, one hears. The names I heard resonated with my monastery teachings and further reassured me about the state I was in. Dr. Yoon sounded like Dr. Jung. Several patients admitted at the same time as I, and who were to be very helpful later, bore the names of important people in my life—Maggie, Richard, Michael, Linford. All had been guides before and were so now also. Such are the gentle touches of the Spirit.

I had lost, it seems, all my usual worldly ways. I could not speak except for a few words—"great" or "beautiful," customary words of mine which the nurses then gave back to me. I had to be taught to eat and had at first no table manners. The simplest things, such as dressing myself, I did not know how to do. But I was not afraid. I felt cushioned, surrounded, sustained by the Spirit of God. I had been in deep prayer on the retreat and had experienced the classical vision of God, a simple earthly form of great significance to me. Gradually, I came out of my totally non-verbal experience with the help of the nurses and the patients I mentioned.

I want to add just a word more about some of the experiences I made there. Our essential beings go somewhere and are very active at night. Normally we do not remember this experience in the morning. In hospital, we all could remember some of these nightly ventures. We could all communicate with each other non-verbally—an inward speech of the heart without external signs. And we could read one another's thoughts.

We also discovered powers of healing, soothing others by just being near them and then leaving when we felt uncomfortable.

All these phenomena are recognized by prayer traditions and belong to the spiritually adept. They are actively sought after. Are they symptoms of sickness? Psychiatry calls them that. We patients all felt deeply privileged and knowledgeable and saw at once that our experiences were of a reality far superior to that known to the medical staff. I tried to keep these ideas of reality, which dove-tailed completely with those of the monastery, separate from the ideas of normalcy which were being projected upon me by the staff. All of us who had arrived about the same time—and could find each other because of the johnny shirts and bathrobes—were very aware of Christ, even if we were not identifying with Him. My life had been centred on Him for the past several years, and I had never felt closer to Him that at that time. When I met Richard, he said to me: "I am your next saviour." Quietly we spoke to one another of God. Not, of course, so that the nurses could hear. We were all having an intense spiritual experience of our inner natures, our true selves.

By now I had come to know the ways of the Spirit as taught at the monastery, ways I set forth in my ESSAYS. I relaxed and let the Spirit put my life together through feeling and impulse. When I felt panicky, someone would be there. When others needed help or a kindness, I would be there. We all ministered to one another's needs with discernment much deeper than anything mind can give.

Difficulties came at the end. Dr. Yoon determined that I must go to my parent's home in Toronto though I did not consider that home at all. I was equally determined to stay in my new home, Nova Scotia.

When I told her that God wants me in Nova Scotia, she must have thought she had a mad woman on her hands. A nurse told me that I had no idea of what reality was—why does the psychiatric profession always think it has a monopoly on reality? I replied to the nurse that I knew far more about Reality than she did. Finally, my sister Janet came down from Toronto to fetch me. She convinced me that I should go home to Toronto to think things over. Her reasonableness prevailed and I left, fearing that I was not ready to face the outside world. As it turned out, I left at the perfect time—another gift of the Spirit. I was beginning to adjust to the nurses' conception of reality and hence losing my own spiritual sensitivity. As it was, as soon as I left, all the experiences I had made there flooded back into consciousness, and I managed to retain that sense for several years after.

What have I to say about hospitalization as a result of this last experience? For the state I was in, so many things were right about it. There were no locked doors. We were trusted to stay on the ward. Structure was minimal, so different from the Payne-Whitney's rigidly structured life. We were left to minister to one another; no one was forced or pushed—again very different from Payne-Whitney. And the doctor's presence was minimal. At the time, that suited me perfectly. The short stay of eleven days and the meaningfulness of the experience there ended the terrible fear I had had, ever since Payne-Whitney, that I would be hospitalized again. Another healing.

The Spirit is present in strength whenever people are gathered together. This is especially the case on mental wards where all the usual defences and the cerebral powers are lost. People are vulnerable and open, and in this case, caring of one another. Of all kinds of reality I have encountered, *the mental ward and the monastery have the most in common.* There, one makes experience of the Spirit that left-brained consciousness knows nothing about except for occasional odd realizations of coincidence—the very hallmark of the Spirit. Women generally know something about the ways of the Spirit which are given to feminine wisdom. If doctors were not in such a hurry to return their patients to the "normal" world of tables, chairs, cats and dogs, we might learn a great deal of the nature of the spiritual world.

I rested for a month in Toronto, integrating my newly deepened sense of the spiritual side of reality with ordinary life, and then returned to the small town in Nova Scotia where I had most deeply felt the presence of God. I was back in Canada. I was to spend a year alone, assimilating, integrating, and deepening into the new-found sense of my own being and into the truth of God and God's ways with us.

7.

Living in Nova Scotia, 1979-80, 1980-83

I returned to a small town by the sea to live and worship for a year. Never had I spent such a happy year. I thought of myself as a hermit, leading a Carmelite life. I had a very small apartment on the back of a house of Jewish people who became my friends. I was close enough to the sea to hear it from my window and just a block from town. I found a teaching position at a local college and spent my evenings writing in the local hotel.

My solitude was glorious. I was still deep in the experiences of the hospital and lived without much *persona* in the riches of interior life. I was totally free of negativity, having expressed it at the doctors in the first hospital. Since I did not know how much stress I could take, I looked after myself very well, spending long hours lying on my bed ruminating my experiences of Santa Fe, Nova Scotia—brooding, integrating. In this, I was supported by St. John of the Cross who claims that the highest state of life and the one which does most for the world is "idleness with God." I lived with the inner child, and my experience of being back in Canada again and of living alone delighted me. I was high on God.

Initially I saw a psychiatrist to prescribe medication. He was a man in his sixties, semi-retired, who told me he wanted me to know who I was and where I was going (though God only reveals a few steps at a time). He was also determined to disabuse me of my fixed idea (God). I, for my part, had the greatest confidence in God and did not relish a father-figure managing my life. I told him so and saw him just enough to monitor my medication. I was on 75-150 mgs of Chloropromazine a day, and also on Artane.

How could a person who for ten years had been emotionally a helpless dependent, unable to go anywhere alone, now travel by herself and live alone, without friends, in a strange town (something that even the most liberated of feminists hesitates to do)?

It is the Lord. My story is a testimony to the power of the Lord. The Lord is an *experiencable reality.* I have mentioned the Jesus prayer. I developed a very close relationship to Him. To Him alone I could pour out my soul, confiding in Him all my fears, anxieties, hopes and difficulties. I have always been guided by his voice within, which I have heard since I was first prayed over at Pecos. (Others, besides schizophrenics, hear inner voices, and they are common in religious tradition.) He, for His part, listened, advised, and filled me with His love. I know no other way to put it. I never wanted for anything emotionally, for the reality of this love surpasses anything a human being can offer. The Lord, and the smiles of waitresses and store clerks, the familiarities of the day, a few new acquaintances, and the occasional visit to Don. These were enough. *The Lord made me independent.*

Don lived in Quebec City that year, and we visited. In the spring, he came down to Nova Scotia, and we looked for land together. We found a remote log house in the forest of Cape Breton, decided to marry, purchased it, and were married in the fall. I was forty-one. We have been living in Nova Scotia and usually wintering in Quebec City or Toronto ever since, sometimes together, sometimes apart.

For those four years, I lived a life of prayer, simple tasks and writing—truly a Carmelite life at the edge of the world.

8.

Cape Breton Mental Health Hospital, NS, 1983

What I have to say now is the most difficult of all, for two reasons. First, I am going to speak to you of inner experiences, very private, having the utmost significance and meaning for me. These are deeply spiritual in nature and feel like a most precious gift. Furthermore, it is a law of God that one may not reveal religious experience to those who are not ready. That is the meaning of "Cast not your pearls before swine, lest they turn and rend you." My hope is that the medical profession is ready to hear such things. John Gainer, psychologist at the Cape Breton Hospital, tells me that psychiatrists often suspect the reality of inner events of the kind I shall describe to you but that they know little about them. It was his total receptivity and openness to my story which has given me the courage to tell it to you.

It was also one of the sweetest experiences of my life. I was mothered and cared for by very gentle nurses and guided by two of the most sensitive men I have ever met, in or out of hospital—John Gainer and Ash Deshpande (OT). I generally find male-being—especially medically trained male-being—arrogant, hard, and abrasive. To their support I owe the wonderful sense of renewal, expansion, and expression of potential that I am beginning to feel.

Finally, the entire experience that summer was so deep in the providence of God, who knew well the sensitivity of my inner child and the fragility of my being, that I shall try to indicate just some of these aspects in order to witness it to you. I have been led, by God, to more and more refined communities of care.

I shall first describe the experience leading up to the hospitalization, then the details of the event itself, and finally all the inner side of it.

We had been living in our forest home since the end of April, 1983, and throughout the spring and early summer, had worked with friends on a Christmas tree plantation about three miles away. Our work was very physical, clearing and preparing sites, planting, piling brush. We worked eight-hour days, and I found the activity often tiring.

I liked the work, although I felt frustration at not being able to write, having neither time nor energy for it. Finally, in desperation, I began to do a little writing in the evenings and did some on the weekends as well. In all that I wrote, I was able to proceed just so far, and then it stopped. I reached a point, in each case, where I felt that I must turn from Western thought to the philosophies of the East. All these writings were unfinished at the time of hospitalization, and still are, though I feel now that I know just how to finish them. But I felt at the time that I had come up against an inner barrier of some kind.

At the time of hospitalization, my work was tapering off. I was shortening my work week and had begun to think my own thoughts again even while on the work site. I looked forward to having time to myself after having been with other people continuously all spring. I had felt, all during this period, a most ardent longing to be with God. My passions, which were strong, were all directed to Him, another reason to be alone.

I was on 2 mgs. Haldol at the time, and anti-depressants, 50 mgs. of Tofranil, a day. I was also seeing a psychiatrist locally, once a month to monitor the medication.

It all began on a most brilliant full moon on the festival of the Christ. I wondered aloud to Don what gift the Lord would give me on this full moon since these festivals are always powerful spiritual events for me.

I believe it was a Friday night. That evening we drove out for supper at a restaurant. As we drove, I glanced through the day's mail. *MS* magazine had come. I opened it randomly. My eye fell upon a description of a gang rape of a twenty-one year old girl by some men in a tavern.

My reaction was strange and instantaneous. A bolt of energy leapt from the depths of my being to the left side of my head. I felt it affected my brain. It put my left eye out of alignment and for awhile I could not focus. I felt physically sick. This state persisted throughout dinner, but by the end my eyes could focus again, and although I felt inwardly awry, we went home.

That night I took a bath and just reclined on the couch for the first time in weeks. I sank into my inner being in a semi-meditative state, little different from other times, though I had a strong sense that I was being prepared for an inner trial. I turned inward. But this time, contrary to other occasions, I did not come out. I do not remember events very clearly after that. I remember encountering something fearful and giving a little cry, at which Puss jumped down from her perch nearby. But generally I felt very peaceful and relaxed. I tried out many yoga poses with Don's assistance. And I felt the presence of God all about me in a great sea of love.

Don is not easily alarmed by my spiritual ventures and was not this time. When I persisted in this state of semi-flaccid paralysis, he finally asked me if he should take me to hospital. I said "yes."

We went to the small hospital in Inverness, about an hour's drive away. I remember the ride, a sense of being immersed in a beautiful darkness and being utterly safe and cared for. Don told me later that I was quite peaceful.

At Inverness, the doctors thought I looked dehydrated and put me on intravenous fluids. I was very gentle and cooperative. I slept a lot of the time. They let Don stay with me night and day, and he slept on a cot in my room. I remember very little of that time, only waking up in a hospital bed and having inner images of what was happening to me. All the images were signals to me that my soul was being finely honed and purified.

Inverness had no facilities for a condition like mine. I was transferred to Sydney, about two hours away. I arrived heavily sedated and was met by Dr. Munshi, who asked me to sign myself in. He saw my reluctance and asked me with the utmost gentleness if I had had difficulties with doctors before. I nodded "yes," and then was able to sign. I remember writing my signature deliberately and boldly because I wanted him to know there was nothing really wrong with me.

I was heavily tranquillized at first. People around me who saw me admitted said that I was in a "dreadful state." No doubt I appeared very withdrawn, and we are all so frightened of not acting normally. I hope my rapid return to the world will inspire them with a faith both in human resilience and medical treatment.

I was put into the admitting ward for seven days where I saw mostly female nurses—the providence of God at that time. I could not have tolerated most men. There was just one other patient on the ward, a very gentle older man. Don was with me every day.

I had a deeply religious sense about what was going on. I saw the nurses as Carmelite saints—especially St. Teresa of Lisieux, the little flower—and so was inspired to respect and trust them, a gift of the Spirit. I remember little of the early days. John Gainer told me that I was having delusions that I had a little boy and must go home to him. The truth was that although I am childless myself, there was a little boy who lived near me whom I have always considered my spiritual child. Even my delusions were really not all that far from ordinary reality.

It was while I was on the admitting ward that I was aware of deep symbols and images for what was transpiring in the depths of my being.

They were all images of undergoing a trial for which I must keep up my spiritual strength and stamina. I shall speak of this later.

The inner images spoke to me of trial, and when I was not focused in physical reality, I was intensely focused in them. Inner experience is as real as outer. I never felt afraid but only surrounded and cushioned with the great love of God coming to me from the people around me. From the gentleness of others.

Twice I heard my inner spirit speak. Once I was standing looking out the window, and I heard it say: "My God, why have you forsaken me"? Instantly a nurse was with me, her arms around me, so deep is the providence of the Spirit. The second time I heard that voice was shortly before I left. It said: "It is finished." These were all words spoken by Jesus during the crucifixion.

One of the female nurses suggested, shortly before I was transferred to the main ward, that I do some painting in occupational therapy. I thought that perhaps I could do this, with her assurance that the man who ran it was "very nice." How important it is to my inner being to have the right words.

So after seven days of much resting and being cared for, I was transferred to the main ward with many other people.

I felt glad to be with people again, but my inner reaction was one of terror. When I saw the men, I heard the little child within me cry out "Rape, rape," and in my mind I saw the many images dating from early childhood of a man exposing himself in the local swamp where I was playing hide-and-go-seek with friends. I always pay attention to that little child and simply used all the techniques I had learned in the Nova Scotia Hospital—staying with other people as long as I felt comfortable, leaving as soon as I felt uncomfortable.

Then, again, the providence of God. So far I had seen no doctors except at admittance. Now I was told I was to see John Gainer. The name seemed right. God often guides me by names. "John" was my father's name. As it happened, Don met him first and they talked. Don, who has a negative opinion of most doctors, told me that John was a good man, a gentle person who could be trusted. He suggested that I treat him as a friend. Oh, fortunate word for a being so sensitive to words! It made me willing to share with John what I was really going through.

With the utmost consideration, John asked me what I would say had happened to me before I came into hospital. I replied that I felt I had come against an inner barrier. Also, I felt that I had been facing incest taboo. Finally, I told him the reaction of my inner child to the men on the ward and of the memory of the man exposing himself when I was four years old. John said: "Perhaps that is the age your passions are."

Then, the following morning I met Ash, the man in OT. That day I was feeling very depressed that I was in a mental hospital again, arriving back to the ordinary world's sense of things. Ash showed me around, and then gave me some paint brushes and paper. I was so eager for them that I was almost rude, and Ash looked at me a little puzzled. I could not wait to be alone. When Ash left me, feelings just burst out of me in paint—small green strokes for my green room, where, as Ash put it later, I was happy. And then the night sky, the moon on the feast of Buddha, the sacred heart of Jesus, and the sea. I named all my paintings. Ash saw me intently at work, and said: "I know. You were going to burst."

And he talked to me about paintings in ways I did not know anyone could talk. How did he know I had a good relationship with the night sky?

Ash saw me. He saw what only one other person has seen in me—the soul of a child. (The other is my Carmelite godmother.) When he saw the determination and logic with which I was painting, he said: "You don't belong here. You belong on the outside." Ash saw that a deeply coherent inner process was at work. As John told me later, they all perceived this immediately and decided to leave me pretty much alone.

The first thing Ash said to me, when he saw my paintings and the way I was painting: "You need to be alone." John Gainer said the same thing. There had been so little time for being alone in the weeks of work just past. As it was, I have never felt happier than being in that room dabbling with paints. Joy returned, and I felt restored to the Lord again.

Ash gave me back my own words for myself—"beautiful," "lovely." He told me: "All your academic work is not really you. You have not yet been yourself." He warned me that I could not just repress my passions. He told me that since he had come to Canada, he had begun to pray. John, too, told me later that I must center my life in God. That is what I am—though the weight of ordinary life and the modern world tells me otherwise.

I could not believe what I was hearing. Doctors who spoke of God! I wanted to dissolve into a happy heap for the sheer joy of it. As it was, I just silently exulted with the Lord. Ash also told me that I was normal, a great reassurance at the time.

I found being in hospital very hard, a great trial. Noise. Too many people. I always could pick up what other people were thinking about me. Since I seem to look a little odd and am sometimes shy, though very likeable when people get past the oddness, at first I found it hard to be with others. I was not told to structure my life or any such thing. John and Ash and the nurses left me to myself. Only toward the end of my stay did the nurses begin to treat me in the ordinary fashion and would, for example, come to my room every time I had gone there to be alone with the Lord. That was the only mistake they made in my stay with them. That is the way I integrate myself, by sharing my experiences with the Lord. But I was also beginning to feel old things from the Payne-Whitney. I feared anxieties would develop. I know now that they develop in me when my deep faith and spiritual sense is threatened by other people's misguided sense of "reality." In much trepidation, remembering how my attempts to broach the subject of leaving had been treated in New York, I told John of my thoughts that I wanted to leave as soon as possible. He was very willing and gave me a night pass to spend in Sydney with Don, and then a week pass to go home to the forest. I had been in hospital two weeks.

I want to mention just one more of the delicate touches of the Spirit. Before hospitalization, I had been discouraged about my writing. So little of it was published. When I came to myself in that first week on the ward, Don had brought me a most beautiful publication containing my article "The Femininity of God," which had just come in the mail. It lifted my spirits and gave me a wonderful sense of identity. Then, just a day before I was to go home, Don brought me a letter from my friend Fiona who had seen the article and wrote to say how good it was. Confirmation from God that I should keep writing!

These are the major events of my third hospitalization.

Now I come to the inner events.

My stay was laced with powerful images which reassured me that everything was okay and which gave me ideas of what was really happening to me. They were very vivid in the first week when I was in and out of ordinary focus; during the second week, they would surface as soon as I was by myself—that patient lying there so apparently withdrawn and comatose is really intensely focused in inner reality!

I have already mentioned that in each hospital experience I saw the familiar *sic et non* (yes and no) of Descartes that I took to mean higher synthesis was occurring.

I have also mentioned images of a trial. In one of the earliest images, I saw myself lying in a hospital bed with a beloved priest friend, Bob, standing by me. At the other side of the room was an open coffin with a skeleton in it. I knew that the skeleton was me and that I had to bring it to life. This image often reappeared throughout my stay, with the skeleton in different stages of aliveness.

I had images of being lowered into a deep well in a bucket, waiting to be drawn up the other side. Or of sinking down and having to throw a rope over a pole to pull myself up.

These were images of some kind of ordeal I must go through.

Some, at least, of the ordeal, was that all the pain of my life seemed to surface. Again, I saw my beloved priest standing by my bed. This time he was reading over me the *Gospel of St. John* beginning with the words: "In the beginning was the word." I knew that as he read, I could go deep into my inner being without fear because the words of scripture would pull me back.

So I felt pain. I felt the pain of any hurts I had caused to other people along the way. I felt a deep psychological pain at having no children. I felt physical pain, the pain of a hysterectomy due to the early detection of cancer when I was forty. I could feel an aching wound in my stomach. I experienced physically the pain I had put animals through as a student of science. As a teenager I had raised animals and had a great love of them as pets. Later, I became fascinated with how they worked and had joined my contemporaries in dissecting frogs and cats. Now, my favourite little guinea-pig and hamster came forth and laid themselves with tears in their eyes on my dissecting board, to be cut open. How I suffered for them. Modern science has a tremendous reckoning with all that it has done to the innocent. I felt their pain. It is a crucifixion to hurt those you love. One does not dissect one's pets. I also felt an intense, physically diffuse pain all over, especially in my joints. It felt as though my soul were trying to leave my body.

I also had to face, in the depth of my being, a terrifying image of the devil coming from Dante's *Inferno*. This hulking figure sits at the bottom of hell trapped in ice. Dante considered hell to be the absence of all relationship. I tried in hospital to turn him into a cheerful centaur. Now when that image appears, I go skating on the ice and feel sorry for the poor old devil who is so bored down there. For Dante, one can only get to heaven by passing through the legs of the devil. Perhaps this was an image for me.

Another image that came was of my father. During our period of work, Don had been impatient with me for one reason or another and was putting me under more pressure than either of us knew. In the back of my mind I was thinking of leaving him—anything to be alone. Then I saw my father, reminding me in images from "A Man for All Seasons" that I had made a vow and that a vow is something before God. When you make a vow, you hold your soul in your hands. If you do not honour it, your soul will slip through your fingers. Fathers are indeed our guides to God in certain aspects.

The deepest image of all, again, during all aspects of my stay, was of crucifixion. For a Christian, there is no more powerful image with which to identify if you have to go through some ordeal. It makes anything bearable.

I saw myself alone in a garden, at prayer, sweating blood.

But the chief scenario was this: Someone had to undergo crucifixion who knew that death was not the end and that pain and suffering are really nothing at all. Who could laugh at death, snap her fingers at it. In this age, it had to be a woman, in order to show to all men, everywhere, that the harlot and the saint, which they think in their absurd literature to be poles apart, are really one and the same. In this ordeal, she would be aided by her trusted comrades, the Brotherhood of Men who understood her. For as she came closer to the cross, even though she could laugh at it, there would be moments when she would forget, when she would need to be sustained by others, when she would faint and fall. And then, her comrades—John, Ash, Don—would be there to help her. To carry her through the weak spots.

She is disguised as an ugly old prostitute—Mary Magdalene. The crowd has hold of her and is taunting her and teasing her. Her hair is dirty and matted; she wears tattered clothes, and she is heavily pregnant. The crowd taunts her again as if she is scum, vermin, of no account. Then, someone suggests crucifixion. The idea takes hold, and they hustle her towards a cross. She faints, falls—her comrades, disguised, reviving her. Again she faints and falls. So resisting all the way, she is dragged toward it, tortured, nailed to its beam. As the cross is lifted into the air, the baby bursts from her stomach. At that moment, she is transformed. Before them all, she becomes a queenly, most beautiful and saintly woman, the crowd falls on its knees in horror and dismay at what it has done. She looks around, and with a faintly bored air, turns to one of the Brotherhood who is standing near her and says: "Now, would one of you fellows please help me down"?

She had shown, even the Brotherhood, what courage really is.

What happened to the baby I do not know.

Hospital, with its noise and people, besides what I was experiencing inwardly, is a tremendous ordeal for me. Images of this process surfaced at different times, and when I was afraid, Don, Ash and John were always sustaining me with their words and reassurances. Toward the end I saw great light within me, inwardly heard Beethoven's *Ninth Symphony*, the *Ode to Joy* and glimpsed the transparent, radiant Christ of Salvador Dali's *Last Supper*.

Then, as if I were a small child, I heard my father's voice as he bent over my crib: "Darling, did you really think we would want a crucifixion"?

These were the images. I also heard words—"this is the steep flight of the alone to the alone,"—from Plotinus, the neo-Platonic philosopher who claims that the center of all things is the One and that one must cut away everything to reach it. "The flight of the alone to the alone."

In the midst of all these experiences, I glimpsed a glory so great I did not know if I could go on living afterwards.

If I had stayed on any longer in the hospital, I would have forgotten these inner sides of my experience. As it was, I came out and wrote them down. They sustained me and supported me, and filled me with the right attitudes at the right times—trust, confidence—as when I had to ask about signing out.

What was really going on? I mentioned the real damage I felt which had occurred when I opened and read *MS.* magazine some two weeks earlier. I was overtired from work. But God works all things to the good of those who love him, and I knew from St. John and St. Teresa that everything happens at once on all levels. As St. Teresa noted: Just when your ways of prayer are changing—as if you do not have enough trouble—God will send you a bad spiritual director. My spirit had felt strong, ready for some new adventure. Both Don and I felt that I had been through some tremendous inner ordeal. We both marvelled that the soul could stand it.

I hope what may have been accomplished in me is a very great healing of my inner being. Healing and clearing out. All that pain was there, now it has surfaced, and I no longer think of it. The clue I have that something of this nature was happening comes from my Carmelite friend in Santa Fe. She wrote to me shortly after I was discharged from hospital. I quote: "Your letter came today, and the account of your mysterious inner experiences while in hospital. There is much in the spiritual life that defies analysis, and St. John of the Cross mentions that sometimes souls are brought to the edge of sanity in the process of being purified. I know of one such person, and she is the only one I would suspect of being in 'transforming union.' The last stage of her night of the spirit was also a trip to a psychiatric hospital where she went through a veritable agony—physical, emotional, spiritual. But she *eventually* emerged truly transformed. She is totally without fear now, whereas previously she was a very fear-ridden person. She is so surrendered to God, as peaceful as a child...I have long been awed by her total generosity and self-gift. She is an intelligent, well-educated woman, like yourself, Lorna, and as simple as a child—a beautiful person, as you are. God doesn't always choose to reveal the meaning of these mysterious events of our lives."

This is to suggest that this experience was really a high event in my life of prayer rather than an "illness," a term which has just the wrong and negative connotation. I was glad when John told me that I had had a psychotic episode and that no one quite knew what that was. The key word of the description of the nun, for my case, must be "*eventually.*" I live in hope that this is what happened.

I want to say one last word about the hospital. I mentioned the great sensitivity I found there. This may be an Eastern influences. Dr. Mian, head of the hospital (who prescribes the lowest doses possible because "all medications have side effects"), Ash, and Dr. Munshi, who met me on arrival, are all from India. Again, another resonance with images dear to my own soul. I always wore Indian blouses.

All these events are mysterious, even awesome, to me. I by no means understand quite what went on, nor does anyone. I know that the greatest pain coincided with the greatest providential love and that these experiences which have a natural and ordinary side have a spiritual dimension as well. There is a wisdom deep at work in us which knows just what we are going through and how much we can take; it puts all the events of our lives together in a unity for us and heals and makes whole. Into the fathomless depths of Its nature, we have only glimpses.

After this last hospitalization, I was eager to be out of hospital and home again in solitude and silence. I continued to paint and saw Ash occasionally and John Gainer once a week. Even though God had sustained me entirely during this experience, when I looked back over it, I was very nervous about Him and about all things religious, and was happy, following the suggestions of the doctors, to just admit the ordinary meanings of life and forsake for a time my austere contemplative self. It was good just to be in the ordinary world. I felt in body and soul that I could not take any more. Often, I felt pain throughout my body and was sensitive to temperature changes and to anything abrasive against my skin.

In my visits to John, he always tried to make me see myself, to see my differences from other people and to cherish these differences. He reminds me often that God is the centre of my life and must be so and that when I wander away from God I get into trouble. It still amazes me that a psychologist would say this! He pointed out to me that the most difficult thing for me is being with other people. He makes me increasingly aware that I am at home in the undifferentiated world of ideas and images rather than in the practical world.

Born under the sign of the fish, I readily navigate the depths where others would lose their way. Even my favourite paintings are those which make others uneasy. Writing and painting are both opening up new dimensions for me. The inner barrier has been crossed, and I am free in some new space. My passions feel youthful and pure, despite the recurrence of the frightening imagery of childhood. God, the passions, and time alone—these must centre and anchor my life. John told me: "Don't get away from God" and "don't change states of consciousness too fast," and "know your needs." He also advised me: Recognize your stresses and raise your medication during them.

I am no longer afraid of mental hospitals or mental illnesses. John has suggested that I regard the hospital as a back-up system to my way of life. This has helped me to attach less significance to it. I do not feel humiliated for being in a mental hospital as I did for years after the Payne-Whitney. On the contrary, I now know that the wards of mental hospitals approach the monastery in making accessible the life of the Spirit. One can make deep experiences of Reality there in a way generally not available in ordinary life. For a Metaphysician, this is of great importance. Indeed, even the popular imagination suspects this, and I have heard jokes to the effect that one day all the truly sane people will be found in mental hospitals. Certainly, in such places one finds people without the masks, deeply in touch with the vulnerability of their own beings and also caring for each other. After one has spent any time in the loving atmosphere of a monastery, life in the world—all camouflaged, structured, armoured—seems ridiculous. So too, from the perspective of a hospital. Modern civilisation is the true psychosis. Abbot David told me once that a psychosis can bring you to yourself and out of your false ways of being.

What have I to add? Now I have shared my inward experiences. I have always been an explorer, a lover of high adventure, a seeker for truth. God has permitted me to explore a territory to which he admits few, to share with Him the deepest adventure of love and knowledge. I am glad to have been able to bring back some of it for others.

9.

Implications of my Experiences for a Theory of the Person and for Treatment

The philosopher and the scientist in me cannot merely share an adventure. They must speculate. And so the question arises of the implications of the experiences I have discussed for (1) understanding what happens in "mental illness"; (2) determining the nature of the psyche; (3) treating mental patients.

First, what really happens in a psychotic episode? In both my hospitalizations in Nova Scotia, I felt that damage had been done to my inward being. John Gainer tells me that the "illness" is thought to be a defence of the ego to an unconscious inruption. There is much too much to face all at once. He also tells me that, chemically speaking, it is a response to a change in dopamine levels.

I have read many other descriptions of what happens and all seem to be to be partially true, as I can verify from my own experience.

Rudoph Steiner claims that thought slips down into feeling. Jungians say that the persona comes off. Primal scream therapists say that a nervous breakdown is the primal scream without a therapist. Morton Kelsey, THE OTHER SIDE OF SILENCE, writing out of a

143

religious tradition, claims that it is an inruption of the unconscious which confers visionary and healing powers. Some say it happens after too much left-brained activity, no doubt why our present civilisation is insane in its treatment of the Earth. R.D. Laing suggests the optimal treatment would be one in which the person will be guided with full social encouragement and sanction into inner space by people who have been there and back again.

My first hospitalization in the Payne-Whitney made none of this possible. I was hustled out of an inner world into a structured life without time to brood, the very thing I needed in my exhausted state.

My second hospitalization in the Nova Scotia Hospital, which seems very enlightened about such matters, was just such a caring, knowing community of people who had all made similar experiences, and my hospitalization was a good, and a very mysterious and exciting, experience.

In my third hospitalization in The Cape Breton Hospital, I found myself even more deeply in inward experience and in an extremely supportive and caring environment. In this state, it is important not to be afraid. Whatever the tranquillizers do, even more is likely done by a patient's own endogenous chemicals which are secreted in response to gentleness, reassurance and trust in the patient. At least this was so in my case. In order to promote such an atmosphere, one really needs to know that the psyche has its own wisdom about these processes, as I believe psychiatrists and others increasingly do know.

I have mentioned the prayer tradition of St. John of the Cross and of St. Teresa of Avila. The higher stages of prayer become experiences that are abnormal by ordinary standards—long periods of inward absorption, inability to enter conversation, almost overwhelming influxes of ideas from the depths.

I have resisted, throughout this work, the term "illness." This is because unless illness is regarded as redemptive—and it is not generally in our culture—it has the negative connotation that one has fallen away from normalcy into an inferior state, an "invalid" state, and hence must be returned to normalcy as soon as possible, "Get well!" From my two perspectives of monastery and mental wards, normalcy, with all its defences, is madness. This is quite different from regarding a psychotic episode as a healing process in itself, as part of a transition to a higher state, and as part of a spiritual path, or as in my case, as a recovery of portions of the personality lost to conscious life. I would urge the psychiatric profession to consider this distinction in order to remove from mental illness the stigma attached to it.

Whatever really happens, it seems clear that in psychotic episodes and perhaps in other forms of "mental illness," one makes an experience of the very depths of one's being, possibly for some healing purposes. Can we say anything of what lies in these depths?

Second, of the psyche, Heraclitus, a Greek philosopher of 500 B.C. wrote: "One would not find out the boundaries of soul by travelling in any direction, so deep a measure does it have."

What is the structure of the psyche? I am not familiar with current psychiatric thinking. The only theories I know are those of Freud and Jung. It seems clear that the active imagination described by Jung played a part in my case. John and I have discussed the hydraulic models of the person and feel that they are not really adequate.

Probably the best books about the nature of our interior being and its depth are by Jane Roberts, or rather, by a personality called Seth who is "no longer focused in physical reality," who speaks and is channelled through her. I recommend them to the medical profession as probably the most provocative and rich account of the psyche that we have— SETH SPEAKS and THE NATURE OF PERSONAL REALITY. Seth claims that consciousness is very deep and that at our deepest levels we have access to knowledge of the planet, of re-incarnational pasts, of other historical periods, and of non-physical systems of reality. (I remind you that Edgar Cayce, a psychic living in the first part of the twentieth century, used to diagnose and prescribe for patients while he was in a trance, although he had no medical knowledge, and that while in trance, he gave an account of the missing years of the life of Christ (JESUS AND HIS CHURCH). Seth urges us to explore and know our full dimensions but warns that when one does this, one loses the ability to function easily in the physical world. Likewise, when one makes a deeply inward Ignatian retreat over *Scripture*, one must usually take some time for re-entry into the ordinary world.

It seems to me that what we can say with certainty about the nature of the psyche is that it is deep and that barriers between its parts are probably not at all as rigid as implied by recent theory. Hence we can move rather easily from one level to another.

Freud gave us the unconscious and discovered that there is rationale and logic in even the most irrational behaviour. Jung has given us in the concept of the active imagination, an interpretation of myths and the part they play in coming to identity. He has also given us a rich set of categories—anima, animus, shadow, persona, Self—for ordering the psychic experience. Seth gives us much information about the organizing center of the person, the soul, which is out of sight. And tranquillizers have emptied the hospital wards.

What I want to add to these accounts are the insights of the spiritual tradition. According to this tradition, the living God dwells in the depths of the psyche and will come to one out of those depths in prayer. Indeed, the church holds that the entire trinity indwells.

I want to suggest, further, that all that happens is part of the will of God, "mental illness" included, and that it must be looked at as though He is playing a part in it. Chloropromazine is part of the story; a wholly merciful, loving, and wise God is the other.

This brings me to the **third** implication—that of treatment of "mental illness" on the basis of an understanding of what is really going on.

I have mentioned the Aesculapian tradition that illness is redemptive, that one must be ill to know the gods. Something was wrong in my case, I was over-tired, dehydrated, over-extended; I had been neglecting prayer.

But *Scripture* has it that "all things work together for good for those who love God." St. Teresa writes that all conditions merge together on all levels.

We can see this in my case. If something was amiss in my situation something also was momentously right. My spirit felt strong (it generally is, and I have difficulty knowing the limits of my body), and I felt well, pleased with my work and ready for some new strenuous adventure. The letter from my Carmelite godmother gives me hope that all that happened was, in God's providence, part of a dark night of the Spirit, an experience in prayer life which is both purifying and healing. When I left the hospital, I felt renewed and healed. I had faced something in the depths and had come through.

To implicate God in the process of "mental illness" is to make it very mysterious. It also suggests methods of treatment which perhaps even now the profession is discovering for itself. To admit God is to admit that a highest providence is at work in what is happening and suggests that we do not impose on patients our own feeble notions of health but encourage them to co-operate with this providence and work with it to recover at their own pace. The less medical interference, the better. My images were immensely healing and sustaining. I think, given my experience in the Nova Scotia Hospital, that many patients have such experiences in the early stages of their hospitalization but forget them later as recovery proceeds.

My experience suggests that healing is a process of co-operation between physical, emotional and spiritual levels. The natural rhythms of a patient should be respected. God knows just what a patient is ready for and how fast the pace should be. Patients really need support and encouragement to trust themselves. I mentioned the fact that I was left largely to myself, except for a few over-zealous nurses. I think if I had been interfered with in any other way, I would have developed anxiety.

As it is now, every day I feel stronger and have a whole new dimension of creative life which I did not have before but which I had been yearning for. If doctors would respect this process and not rush their patients back to ordinary life but try to find out more about it, we might indeed come, on all levels of life, to a knowledge of the ways of the Spirit which is normally to be had only in monasteries.

If a patient can be encouraged to trust the images and to put herself in the care of the all-wise Divine physician, she may be able to relax and let the interior being gather itself together at its own rate. Far from the stigma now attaching to hospitalization for "mental illness," this time might come to be seen as a time of privileged contact with God and with one's own ultimate reality. The popular imagination already suspects this.

My experiences suggest that God, or one's true centre, is at work in a psychotic episode, not merely the unconscious or ego defences. They suggest that one is not merely ill but that one is on the way to a higher synthesis. They incline us to be hopeful and optimistic about what has happened because what was true for me may be true for all.

In the words of Abbot David: "Even in the most expensive hospital in New York, the way down is the way up."

Afterword

I finished this work in October, 1983; it is now March, 2003. I have not been hospitalized for twenty years.

I still live as a writer-contemplative in the world, walking easily with two senses of reality, the ordinary Cartesian sense, the spiritual sense. I live part-time in Canada, part-time in rural US Southwest. I love best the holiness of the ordinary. My difficulties come with the transition between the two worlds. I handle transitions by putting God on hold and erring on the side of the ordinary.

I am now sixty-three. I have puzzled about the Payne-Whitney all my life. What went wrong there? Why were they so ineffective in my case?

They missed me at the beginning. That is when a lot of hospitals and patients miss each other. The patient arrives, afraid and confused—since most people have never experienced the collapse of your personalities—hospital personnel have no idea how terrifying this is—and is promptly met with threats, restraints and needles. This can scar one for life.

In my case, it was none of these things, but they destroyed my trust in them almost immediately. What happened to me? I came very open, wanting and needing safety and help. But they began by telling me that everything I most prized, about my life and my large, exuberant and unusual self, was wrong.

What happened? I saw the traditional notion of "normalcy"—how I despise "normalcy"—being foisted upon me and I withdrew into fear and terrible, crippling anxiety.

When my strength and health began to return, and my usual exuberance, I was met with hostile disapproving looks from both staff and patients so that I did not feel safe anywhere. To this day, I have great difficulty in knowing how to present and "manifest" my own essence to others.

A friend said: "They applied their technology to you and when that failed, they didn't know what to do."

I can forgive the Payne-Whitney what it did to me. Indeed, I take responsibility for what happened there. If I could have summoned up my courage to see a minister, it might all have turned out differently. I could have spent the time learning and at prayer.

But it is more difficult to forgive them what they did to my mother.

My parents drove down from Canada to see me in hospital. They were told by the young doctors—the Payne-Whitney is a teaching hospital—that they could not see me because "Lorna's family is her problem."

My "problem!"

I had finished a difficult thesis in science, a beloved professor with whom I was going to study that year had died, I was reading alone Kant's THE CRITIQUE OF PURE REASON, I had fallen in love with Don, my first love since teenage years, and they picked on my family.

My doctor was a woman doctor. She was also a mother; she should have known better. As it was, that callous word, said at the wrong time, destroyed forever my mother's life. She was sixty at the time; her family had been her whole creation, her pride and joy. The doctors told her, in essence, that her whole life was a failure.

On the way home to Canada, caught in a motel in a snowstorm, my mother experienced her first nervous breakdown. She has lived with no sense of self-worth in the thirty years since, has been hospitalized many times for severe depression, and even when she was 92, in a retirement home, she suffered from terrible depression and guilt at being "a bad mother."

My family! We were close-knit then and continued to be so.

I still marvel that a group of young men and women fresh from medical school expected me to betray my family to them.

But then, Freud never mentioned loyalty.

The young doctors.

They said just the wrong word at the wrong time.

But then, Freud never said anything about compassion.

Oh yes, the confident young doctors. They, of course, know all about the soul; they have read the textbooks.

I still marvel at the inhumanity. Well, the Payne-Whitney is a teaching hospital and this is the problem everywhere with modern medicine, its lack of humanity. I forgive the Payne-Whitney.

May I never have to be hospitalized again in "the most expensive hospital in New York." I would take a little local regional hospital far from the big city centres, which still knows vestiges of humane common sense, any day.

How is it with me now? I live in God and go from miracle to miracle in the Great Mystery that Spirit is and the incredible journey my soul is making in this life.

Peace.

June 20, 1998

IV.

A Treatise on the First Principle

Knowing, the One, and the Nature of the Universe

Dedicated to Don, the Love of All My Days,

in Sunlight or in Shadow

Table of Contents—Essay IV

They say all my works come from intellect.
This is not true, they come from passion.

—*Matisse*

With Grateful Thanks to Tim Horton's at the corner of Charlotte and Townsend, in Sydney, Nova Scotia, where most of this writing was done.

For My Brothers:

Calvin Normore
Ken Henwood
Peter Timmerman
John Gainer
Don Knight
Michael Jones
Len Brown
Peter Poole
Graham Hitchins

"Your only limitations are spirited ignorance."

—Seth

1.

Knowing

For Calvin, who always coveted the Green soul—the richness of simplicity.

It is one thing to know *what* the universe is, something else to *relate* to it, to *commune* with it.

One thing to know of the reality of God, quite different to take up relationship, to *commune* with the living God.

"We walk in the ways of our ancestors, and that cannot be broken." (Midnight Oil)

"Faith of our fathers, living still, in spite of dungeon, fire and sword."

I have an inner life with God, I know the ways God works with us in the physical world, I work with the world of spirit. My dreams are "God's forgotten language." Now I would go deeper into my Carmelite ways.

My heart sings at the prospect of being in this small town by the sea, deepening my ways with God.

Joy fills me this day.

I had body work yesterday, and my soul is in my body again.

What is life? Joy here followed by joy there.

Joy fills me this day, for I am once more working with the depths, with my own soul.

Last night I met my grandparents!

And the day?

This day is fresh and fair, the grey clouds lifted, grey clouds gone from about my heart.

The day, I cannot have enough of the day.

"Give us this day…"

Mother: "Let's see what the day brings."

Expect the joy, the miracles of God, and you will have them.

I *embrace* Sydney.

Most of what I know about God I learned from fundamentalists, who are the only ones to take seriously the promises of *Scripture*.

Where am I in my life?

The long years of formation are over; the years of creative maturity begin.

Works done.

I listen for the voice of my own soul.

So many thoughts, august thoughts, the vision, the dream of summer.

How do I feel about my life?

It was always the joy of being about some lofty purpose. Of being "on the way," first to metaphysics, then of union with God, then to Don.

I have time, now what?

In the first instance, my Carmelite path of unpacking/exploring my own soul.

Carmelites *love* being purified of all that is not God.

But then: Harvest time.

The autumn of my life.

There is so much I would see and say, have seen, would say, would craft into shape and form. A life.

I seem, looking back, to have *romped* through it.

It was always joyous, for Don was always there, and I was always learning wonderful things about God.

Now?

At sixty, I feel it's time to settle down, to be faithful to the promises of my youth.

I remember in my twenties, the vision of my life, prophetic seeing of the shape of things to come.

Youth would be interesting.

Middle age would be uneventful. (In fact it was my wilderness life of prayer which has filled me with knowledge of all things.)

The last would be the best, much like my youth.

Strange, to anticipate then, so full a flowering.

*   *   *

Joy in God is always with me.

It is time to get serious.

To employ wisely and well the gift of time.

*   *   *

I have been "*called.*"

"Many are called, but few are chosen."

"Many are the Thyrsus bearers, but few the mystics." (Socrates)

"You have not chosen me, I have chosen you, to bear much fruit that will last." (Jesus of Nazareth)

I have been *called*, through sciences of the day, through all the philosophers, through the great works of the West, to a simple solitary life with God.

It has been a Way, guided by questions and their answers.

The greatest of my questions, in my twenties, was about knowing. *What* could be known? Who are we who could know?

I have answered this question. It has to do with God being consciousness, Infinite Love-consciousness. The universe is essentially formed from consciousness, matter is just consciousness "stepped down," we human beings are "fragments of God," a portion of Infinite Consciousness in a body. Reality is transparent to intellect as Aristotle hoped it would be. And Earth? Earth is a living, conscious, spiritual and divine being who will relate to us.

Truly, "mind has arranged all things for the best." Anaxagoras

I have no other questions.

*   *   *

Parmenides: "Whatever is, is intelligible."

How can this be?

All comes to be from Ideas and is known through Ideas.

It is no accident we take our ideas seriously.

Experience.

Knowledge comes through experience.

The objects of the world come through experience.

So does knowledge of God; that was my great discovery at the monastery of Pecos: All knowledge of God is experiential.

All religion originated in someone's experience.

God.

And then: A life of prayer brings with it *infused knowing*—knowledge of the inner workings of other souls, knowledge of the inner of the universe, knowledge of what God is doing in a life, prophetic knowledge—knowledge that does not come through experience.

By "experience" I mean "through the senses."

Aristotle: "...nothing in the mind which was not first in the senses."

This is not so. God grants infused knowledge never in the senses.

We also have, not just the outer senses, but sublime inner senses of which much of humankind is at present unaware.

What is it to know God, Spirit, invisible and ultimate, through the senses? Ah…

Inward touch.

And love which engulfs us.

*   *   *

The natural world, the spiritual world.

We belong to both, we human beings, as does everything else, every animal and plant, every stone and star.

We are *knowers*, inescapably knowers, designed and made for Truth, physical and spiritual.

"How can I know, even as I am known?" (St. Paul)

We are part of that which knows.

Knowing. I have no more questions. We can know anything, we only know in different ways. We can know our past lives, the depths of our own souls, the nature of the universe, God, but some self-development, some "taking ourselves in hand" is necessary.

I have known by *immersion*, as I learned to swim. (Ken Henwood showed me this.)

I knew modern science by totally immersing myself in it and finding out its limits.

And so for the philosophers, the great books, Catholicism. One can only "know the ocean by being the ocean." (Eastern saying)

So: I knew the ways of each and the limits of all.

We are knowers, inescapably designed for knowledge and truth.

We know in a thousand ways, through our minds, our senses, our emotions, our spirits, our bodies, our souls.

We can know Reality in all its fullness because of what Reality is and because of whom we are.

It is not possible always to put knowledge into words.

"Stop talking and thinking and there is nothing you cannot know." (Eastern saying)

We know.

Nothing is hidden. It reveals itself after time when one is worthy of it.

It is all possible because the universe and ourselves are essentially Spirit, consciousness, and everything else is essentially Spirit, consciousness.

Now I am immersed in God and in my experience of the cosmos.

*   *   *

The keys for me are two fragments of Heraclitus:

> "Listening not to me, but to the *Logos*,
> it is wise to agree all things are one."

> "You would not find out the boundaries of soul
> by travelling in any direction, so deep a measure does it have."

I would add to these, a third:

> "The things of which there is touching and seeing
> and hearing, these do I prefer."

Why?

For an alive, awakened spirit, God travels *on sense knowledge* and the senses are *channels to the living God.*

All knowing comes through touch—to minds, sense, bodies, emotions, spirit, souls.

It comes through receptivity and identification, *becoming one with.*

Abraham knew Sarah; knowing is something like that.

The impulse to know—to relate to, to identify with—is born of deepest Love and brings with it immense Joy.

God, the solitary one, *wishes* to be known.

And so we yearn for God, as God once yearned for us, and all our knowing nests in Spirit, the overarching, the guardian.

Love is first in the universe; the impulse to know is born of Love.

Knowing begins with questions; it ends speechless with amazement, admiration, Joy, and enjoyment.

        *   *   *

My formation has been Greek.

Before Anaxagoras, Parmenides, Heraclitus, is the first philosopher we know about. Thales: "All is water."

Water is very like consciousness, coming as it does in various forms, knowing no absolute boundaries but continuity.

Consciousness: All function with semi-permeable membranes. (Peter Timmerman)

Consciousness is essentially continuous.

My understanding is essentially pre-Socratic.

Thirty years ago, as a student of philosophy in Toronto, I felt that an age had ended, that we were at a whole new beginning in thought, and I sought inspiration in the Pre-Socratic mystics. After that came great books and the religious traditions.

Now?

In my Ending, is my Beginning.

What follows?

That great spirit who wrote "the sun is new each day" was not a primitive astronomer; he knew how to live.

Few suspect just how accessible to us the great powers of God are, but we are fragments of God and anything is possible.

Now *know* and bring the fruits of your knowing back down into the Earth plane, for the good of all.

Knowledge begins in Love and Joy; it ends in Love and Joy.

Now I am so taken up with joy, with simply being alive, that I do not ask quite so many questions. Instead, I live in God and marvel at the *miracles* in my life.

It is one thing to *know* the essence, another to *be* the essence.

July, 1999

"A road opens up in solitude to a Reality so ultimate it disdains to embody itself for sense."—C.S. Lewis

2.

Of Kant and Knowing

For Ken, my little Cornish Cousin:
"I loved you once, Atthis, long ago."
                                    —Sappho

Kant believed in reincarnation. His CRITIQUE OF PURE REASON confined knowing to "appearances" and sketched its limits. Knowledge—especially scientific knowledge—was only "empirically real, transcendentally *ideal*." Into the truly Real, into "noumenal" reality, no insight could be had.

Kant opened the door into the mystery just a crack in his ethical works. Here, the *fact* of the *existence* of ethics enabled one to assert *also* the *conditions* of ethics—the existence of God, freedom and immortality—which Kant for various reasons thought to be the necessary conditions for ethics at all.

Kant's entire "Copernican revolution" began because he wondered at the steady sure progress of science, whereas in theology, thinkers disagreed, and hence no sound knowledge could be had.

Kant never read the mystics. If he had, he would have marvelled at the tremendous *agreement* among them concerning both *experience* of God, and God.

Men of mind and reason know nothing about God who is "beyond" and "outside the physical domain—the territory of mind.

God is given only to those who tap into the internal depths of their own souls, to those who through prayer, meditation or natural ability "know the ocean by being the ocean."

To those who enter the inner realms of *pure consciousness*, "the kingdom of the Rishis."

East Indian mystics have always known, from *direct* experience, that the essence of the universe was *consciousness*. This is the step Kant failed to take.

If Kant had been able to take this last step, that *we* are more like God than "objects," the knowing of which had been a preoccupation of the tradition before him—if he had been able to take this final step of learning from human nature and to assert that God, the divine nature, consciousness, i.e. "noumenal reality," was simply *consciousness*, barriers would have fallen, and he might have known the whole truth. What is the full truth? This:

God is Infinite Consciousness

The entire universe is formed of and *is* essentially consciousness, love-consciousness at that.

The universe functions according to teleological principles, is loving, creative and intelligent throughout, hospitable to every creature that inhabits it.

We and everything else are portions of Infinite Consciousness in a body, attuned to our niche in the physical.

Matter, the physical universe, is simply consciousness "stepped down" as it were and is supported and maintained by forces from deep within the greater and more ultimate spiritual world.

The "conditioned, finite and temporal rest on the unconditioned, infinite, eternal." (The Buddha)

All the true laws of the universe are *principles of consciousness*, love-consciousness and joy at that.

The physical world is an "appearance," a camouflage over the Real.

We can know the Real because we are part of the Real.

We can know God by direct experience.

We can *commune* with the source of the universe.

The true ends of life are joy "here" and then joy "there."

Reincarnation is the way the universe functions and justice prevails.

We can affect the universe through prayer and *intent.*

Our true "I Am" *is* the Real *par excellence.*

There are corollaries to this view of the universe:

Time is an illusion, part of the "rules of the game" for inhabiting the physical world; in truth all happens simultaneously.

Space, time and matter are, as Kant thought, not ultimately real; they are empirically real only.

There are infinite spiritual worlds and systems of reality.

Kant's Copernican revolution involves the *knower* and the *known,* considered to be *objects.*

Essentially, Kant reversed the priorities in knowing and determined not what the *object* contributed to knowing but what the *knower* did.

He began his enquiry with a particular model of the human: *Mind in a body knowing things.* (Bequeathed by Descartes)

He never got beyond his model except in ethics, where he discovered, in us, something not "of the world" appearing "in the world," namely the *Categorical Imperative.*

God was not present in Kant's model at the beginning and could not really get in at the end.

What I have affected here is a much more radical Copernican revolution than Kant's. It is to stand modern science on its head.

The core assumptions of modern science are that matter is first in the universe, the universe materially evolves, and consciousness appears only at the end of the process when matter reaches "a certain state of complexity" in the human alone.

No complexity of matter will ever form consciousness!

Near-death experiences prove—and this is *the* crucial experiment for *all* modern science—that consciousness is separable from matter. Patients report finding themselves out of their bodies hovering near the ceiling, looking down at the doctors working over them, able to read dials—later confirmed by doctors—they could never have seen from the position of lying in their beds.

In short, we can see without eyes, hear without ears, and think without brains.

And so, I challenge the modern assumption that all comes to be from matter—and it is an assumption—and *reverse the dependency* to say:

Consciousness comes first and matter second.

This is the true Copernican revolution.

It is to see as God sees, not from our limited standpoint, but from God's.

And then it is to say how this is possible, as I have here.

We are *knowers*, inescapably designed for knowledge and Truth.

The universe is *transparent to intellect*, as Aristotle hoped it would be. Why? Because the universe is a spiritual being, and we are spiritual beings.

*   *   *

These conclusions have ramifications for every department of knowledge and human affairs.

They have especially ramifications for our *lives on Earth*. For what is the Earth? Earth is a living, conscious, spiritual and divine being. So is every inhabitant on her, as conscious and spiritual as we are, yearning for true relationships with us, heart to heart, Soul to Soul.

God is *in the Earth* and may be experienced there.

Earth and her inhabitants are "God under a thousand forms," as the *Bhagavad-Gita* recognizes.

Earth and all her inhabitants are *sacred* and need to be respected as such.

Earth is *primary* here, *we* are secondary—another Copernican revolution. We need to curb our destructive practices upon her if we would be here long-term.

We came "down from heaven"—i.e., the spiritual world—*in order to be here*. We need to bring our spiritualities down to Earth and bring the joy, the love, and the wisdom of the spiritual plane into the Earth plane.

We are all immortal. Existence is glorious.

And what is ethics really? The appropriate: *The tip of the iceberg of love.*

We are meant to be co-creators with God, using our powers of prayer and intent, of a viable, happy, and joyous civilization on Earth.

August, 1999

3.

Metamorphoses:
Where Are We Now?

For Peter Timmerman: "Spirit is empty and waits on all things."
—Lao-Tzu

The whole of human history, the way people behave, can be understood as evolving interpretations of what God wants and does not want, what God enjoins and prohibits. "Many are called, few are chosen." I speak as Prophet: We are at the turning point.

This is, these times, the times of the Second Coming of Christ, *the* turning point of history, the ending of one historical day, an ancient dark, brooding and painful historical day, the winter of the human race and the beginning of another, our Springtime on planet Earth, the emerald planet.

It is the ending of one great historical day, the beginning of another.

Winter and Springtime.

So: She who says these things to you was born on February 28th, symbolically, the last day of the winter months. I incarnated in 1939 because I wanted to experience the winter of the human race before it entered its springtime.

There are no accidents in this magical universe of ours.

We are in the transition from the Piscean Age to the Aquarian.

From ages of fear and separation, to a new age of love and connectedness.

From an age (the two fishes) of the dualistic consciousness of Being to an age of the unity consciousness of Being.

From an age of mind and reason to an age of the heart and to a whole new relationship to the unconscious and spirit who dwells there, symbolized by the sign of Aquarius, a human figure carrying a pitcher of water.

We leave behind us an age of churches; we enter an age of spiritual practice, a spirituality without churches or authorities where each person chooses the path most appropriate to them.

We leave behind the Western tradition of thinking—of finding God, with Plato, "high in the head," up in the sky, in Heaven—for a renewed relationship with the Earth, the body, and the God who is in the Earth, here in us, in the ground beneath our feet.

It is no accident that she who says these things bears the name Green and has experienced many native life times before this.

We are fragments of God, a portion of God in a body.

And what are spiritual practices?

Those which allow us to develop our full size, all our buried and hidden inner abilities, our abilities to know the inner of things and relate to each other and the Earth and her inhabitants, all the giraffes and the nasturtiums, pines, rocks and wolves, mosquitoes and ants, with the very fullness of our consciousness and theirs, body, mind, soul, spirit, ALL.

We are the sons and daughters of God, we are embodiments of God, we are all, together with plants and animals and the Earth herself, *incarnations of the living God.* It is time to be Real, for we are larger than we have realized and contain in our "within," where dwells the pure essence of Spirit—powers and abilities that our long-ago and distant ancestors had but which we have lost along the way of history.

We are meant to be large, deep, full and in our own power.

And this is the new meaning of God.

God wants to come to Earth; God wants to be God in us, fully embodied, fully alive, fully grounded. God wants us to bring spirit to Earth, to live here as though we meant to stay here, and to realize the ways of God—peace, love and joy—on Earth and to bring the wisdom and love of the spiritual world from whence we come *here* to Earth.

Our only limitations are spiritual ignorance, and it is this which lies at the root of all our problems.

God wishes us to be in our own power, and what power that is if we are fragments of the living God!

And sex, which the old God thought demeaning and despicable?

Highly approved of, in all aspects, ways, kinds.

We are meant for joy, to be radiant butterflies rather than little caterpillars.

We owe our freedom to a romance with Ideas. The past is not abandoned but included and overcome in higher synthesis, like Hegel's.

The way of Carmel is an inner way.

August, 1999

4.

Of the Self

For John, true friend of the Holy Spirit:
"You would not find out the boundaries of soul by travelling
in any direction, so deep a measure does it have."—Heraclitus

Self-Portrait:

> Archetypal Woman
> God/The Passions
> Poetry
> Wind/Rain
> Silence

       *   *   *

Contemplative.

What is that?

It is to have a good relationship with the Night Sky, the Stars, the Moon, and all the shimmering divine Earth.

*   *   *

Flowers.

The Pure, Bright, Clear Consciousness of Flowers.

Green Plants.

Children: So alike, so alike.

Woman.

*   *   *

The Infinite
The Finite
The Formed
The Formless

All is one. (Heraclitus)

The beauty of the blue sea.

*   *   *

One fully grown, but having the heart of a child.

Wise Woman.

*   *   *

Planet Elder:

> Earth Dreamer
> Vision Seeker
> North Star

*   *   *

A Wilderness Life:

> Owls
> Mosquitoes
> Black Flies
> Crows
> Blue Jays
> Chickadees
> Ants
> Bees
> Butterflies
> Warblers

*   *   *

Deep Waters
Shining Rivers
Clear Lakes

*   *   *

Night
Morning
Day
Evening
Twilight
Dusk

*   *   *

Ash: "You see beyond."

John: "You see the totality."

The Self

For Plato, the number for the human, the number for human wholeness, was four. For Jung too, this.

My experience in the Payne-Whitney Mental Clinic was that somehow a unity among four elements or aspects had come apart. It never came together for me there.

I follow, consciously, a Carmelite path, that is a path through many intermediate states of soul to "union with God." Actually, all are more or less following such a path to greater or lesser degrees.

St. Teresa describes this as the progression through "seven mansions in the interior castle of the soul, God being in the innermost room." Her claim: We are here to do deeds for God and cannot really do them until we are in union with God in this seventh mansion of the soul. All the mansions are somewhat fluid, and during the course of a life, one comes in and out of union many times.

The mansions can be distinguished by different experiences, and typically, on the threshold of the seventh mansion, one experiences great fear, doubt and purification, great influxes from the depths.

Characteristically, when I am in this transition in the world, I have totally forgotten I am contemplative because I never tell people I am contemplative. I say I am "a writer."

One state of union has to give way for a more advanced state, and for this advanced state to occur, this often feels like coming apart at the seams. One is afraid everywhere, comfortable nowhere.

St. Teresa describes this as "the soul seems to be split in two." This most often occurs in me with a change of place. Looking back, I can see what has happened, in the middle of it, I have forgotten all. That is where I was when I saw you Thursday, deluged by inner life and apart at the seams.

What *is* union?

In my case, it is some profound rearrangement of masculine and feminine within. (This word often comes out as "famine," given the situation of the feminine energies in the modern world. When I saw you I was in pure feminine feeling.

St. John of the Cross describes it as "the strength of armies within, the grace of creatures without.

I begin in feeling; then the masculine principle of Form enters in.

Plato described the soul as tripartite. I suppose it is the tripartite psyche, together with the body, that makes up the four-fold person.

Last night, I dreamt there were three of us, riding a locomotive—me, a young girl, and an older man. We were repelling soldiers who were trying to push us off.

Today I find myself in union. A whole new sense of wholeness and simplicity.

The person has been variously described:

> Reason
> Understanding
> Will
> Emotion
>
> Soul
> Mind
> Emotion
> Body
> Spirit

That is the philosophical understanding. The Catholic understanding is body, soul and spirit, soul being composed of mind and emotions. Then the Platonic understanding: The spirited part, the emotions and reason, the body. For Jung:

> Extraversion/Introversion.
> Intuition/Sensate
> Feelings/Form
> Judgement/Perception

All of this would form a fluid yet stable structure, immensely complicated by particular feelings, thoughts, emotions and all the other delights of inner life.

Union always takes some time to settle down, to "gel" as it were. And it takes place in the world, amid the speaking of languages, the doings and going places of the day, which can enormously complicate my sense of what is *really* happening.

We live in a universe basically formed of consciousness in which all functions by intelligence, as an interconnected whole, an Order permeated by intelligence.

There is order of some kind of inner chaos.

But sometimes, one needs a steadying hand.

Mother Rose: "Lorna, try to trust God completely."

*　　　　　*　　　　　*

Every culture in the world makes mandala as an emblem of human wholeness, but a wholeness of what element? I do not know.

In my case, the very ultimate four of the union is a unification of my highest spiritual consciousness, Christ conscious, with the Masculine and Feminine elements in a new balance, with inner child alive.

The Unconscious

We are deep on our inner side. The unconscious is the unknown.

The physical world is a projection from deeper, spiritual worlds. On our inner sides, we open into those spiritual worlds, and spiritual paths—Eastern, Western and North American Indigenous work with these worlds.

Who is the shaman?

One who mediates the divine to the human.

An intermediary.

Jesus Christ was a great shaman.

Our spiritual powers lie in the *inner* of our beings, where we connect with all in a universe which is essentially consciousness despite the apparent "separateness of bodies."

Consciousness knows no boundaries.

It is simply amazing in all of this that we can keep our balance.

The inner world; the outer world: One.

"There are no accidents."

Women are said to be closer to the unconscious than men.

We access spiritual worlds through our Feminine functions.

And before God, even men are anima.

We have our body to counterbalance the soul.

$$*\qquad\qquad*\qquad\qquad*$$

It is one thing to describe it, another thing to live the descriptions.

This is why people describe themselves as their *doings in the world* and not their beings. Indeed, "you would not find out the boundaries of soul by travelling in any direction, so deep a measure does it have." (Heraclitus)

Psychologists and psychiatrists deal with the Soul and by extension the whole Universe.

We inhabit intersections:

The Infinite/The Finite
The Formed/The Formless
The Eternal/The Temporal

We live in a between.

We dwell in mystery.

>Mystic: One conversant with the Mysteries.

>Metaphysics: The wisdom of ultimate things (the Goddess of which is Athena).

>Sophia: The wisdom principle who spoke through Jesus Christ (feminine).

>Psyche: The soul (feminine).

Strange how many terms are falling into fours.

I am one well acquainted with the Night.

Beauty is the one form which shines "here as it does there." (Plato)

Beauty puts us in direct connection with the Divine.

I Am.

The soul needs images of itself.

I like mine best, steeped in the divine dark living waters of prayer, at peace, so like the night sky with little silver fish, swimming in and out.

Today I see colour.

I prefer the model of the cone, which first came to me on a holiday in Nova Scotia when I was twenty-nine.

The tip of the cone is our anchorage in present events; a little lower down are our memories of yesterday, our lives; further down, are reincarnations, the memories of the Earth, and on down into the deep spiritual webwork and networks of the universe. And God.

St. Teresa's Prayer of Quiet: Her Centre is on the centre of the universe. Thus may other spiritual beings channel through us.

I am a deeply cleared being. I would hear God out.

*   *   *

I am painting mandala. The first mandala I ever made was on a retreat in the Jemez Mountains of New Mexico before coming to Nova Scotia in 1979.

I was very close to God; I asked for a mandala, expecting something with geese and trees. Instead, what instantly came into my mind was a *mandala of the relationships* that I must work with. Mother and father; John and Janet; Timmy; Don. I have worked with these. The next mandala came in 1983 just before I ended up in hospital. Three corners—a cat reclining on a cushion, two ducks in reeds, my green canoe surrounded by reeds. The fourth came in during my stay in hospital—two loons swimming by a cliff with a pine tree over it.

It was a mandala of words, and in the centre of this mandala were four concentric circles. The mandala was one of words, of what can be said to whom. God's mysteries can be said to all, women's only to women, Lorna's only to friends, and Buddha mysteries—all the little touches and glances and glimpses of God may be said to no one.

I have not made any since. Now?

Now, I go to write in my little coffee shop.

I am a student of language, an over-hearer of conversations, one sensitive to the magic and beauty and power of words, as was my mother, who was nourished on Shakespeare.

I can conclude there are four major languages for comprehending reality—or at least designating it and navigating within it—in order of degrees of ultimate truth:

> The Spiritual
> The Intellectual
> The Emotional
> The Physical

They are all embodied in the beautiful wonderful, to be honoured and treasured, incarnate languages of the day and reflect the traditional spiritual sense of the four aspects of human wholeness: Spirit, mind, emotions, body. Health is the well-being of all.

The ultimate and final standpoint on all things is the categories of spirit, of spiritual understanding invoked at life's major passages and on momentous occasions. (Frieda Lastrus) I love to hang loose in the rich waters of my own soul and live my joy in God, let God put my life together and just marvel at and rejoice at all the miracles. Now, I am back in the present, firmly grounded and rooted here.

The marvellous power of the Now in which all our aspects, words and systems of reality come together, and we are One, ravelled up, whole, in a place beyond all categories and concepts.

*   *   *

Saints and sages have always welcomed old age.

*   *   *

Who are we then?

Portions of God—Infinite Consciousness—in a body.

On our near side, we are focused and specialized and adapted for functioning in the physical plane of existence; on our far sides, we deepen into the infinite and into cosmic consciousness.

What holds us together?

Our divine "I Am," which mediates between and among all Worlds, all Systems of Reality.

We are spirits nesting in that greater spirit, the love-consciousness out of which the universe comes and is formed. Lovers and thinkers all, voyagers through a mystery. "On a journey every step is appointed." (Elie Wiesel)

That love, wisdom and will, which is the Universe, manifest themselves in our lives as what the ancients call providence; all our needs are sublimely met.

I call it magic.

*   *   *

"And the solitude of the Ages shall be established in her. Deep wisdom at work in us, far, far beyond the reach of the conscious mind."

"The soul is an *entity*, best named when it names itself. It has a Centre."

Behold, the centre holds in small things and in great.

God is with us.

I Am.

*   *   *

"…fearfully and wonderfully made" (Shaman)

And so I say of the infinitely deep self that it is composed of these elements

> An intelligence which is far greater than mind,
> An organizing centre,
> A principle of unity,
> An inner boundary, which is sometimes crossed,
> Body/soul.

Completed for John Gainer just after the full moon of the Christ (on which I ended up in Cape Breton Hospital in 1983 for two weeks).

June, 1999

5.

Of the One

*For Don, First Snow: "God comes to us
through Beauty, the one Form which
shines **here** as it does **there**."*
　　　　　　　　　　　　—Plato

The greatness of the morning light.

My mind bows this day, before great death, who once again draws near. "Sister Death." (St. Francis of Assisi)

My brother-in-law's brother Clive, sixty-eight, two years older than John, died last night from a lung cancer.

And this week my "mission" to the Earth begins in simplicity, in obscurity, in anonymity.

*　　　　　　　　*　　　　　　　　*

Touched once again by the Forms. (Plato)

Plato: We are born into a particular society, put on its blinkers, and after a long time functioning within it, come to maturity and *take them off.*

For what?

For greater knowing.

For original knowing.

The knowing of the child who has ripened within us and is now fully grown.

Original knowing.

So, a beggar leapt over the wall of the garden where the scholarly Rumi was teaching and, throwing his scrolls and manuscripts into the fish pond and gazing fiercely into his eyes, said: *"Now will you teach what you know"*?

The rest of Rumi, the utterances which have come down to us, are what Rumi, the mystic, knew.

We know, we *all* know, we are inescapably knowers, designed for knowledge and truth.

We are born into a world of "things"—tables, chairs, dogs and cats—the Cartesian world of matter. The weighable, the extended in space and time.

And the belief structures of our civilization geared to "this world."

We grow apace in this, as sons and daughters, students, teachers, parents in our turn.

In the midst of all this, we have a "presentiment, an inextinguishable desire for realities having the greatest significance for us, but beyond our ken." (Kant)

I came to the One *through* the world of objects and the belief structures of the day. In the world of objects, spirit is a problem. We *think* we know objects, and we think we know how we know.

The positivist, in all of us, takes objects to be all there are, materialism is the only creed which promises to "keep the bogeys" out. (C. S. Lewis)

But it keeps out angels too.

I came to spirit among things, and now, it seems to me that I knew it all along and was simply prevented from recognizing *It* for the clutter of thoughts in my own mind.

Now my mind is clear of thoughts, I like it that way, my path of kenosis piety; I live beyond categories and all but the simplest speech.

How pathetic seems our little thingy world of cars and coffee cups, tables and chairs

Things come into existence, they go out of existence, they break, they decay.

So Aristotle felt the need of a Prime Mover in order to keep them moving in their desire to attain its perfection.

The more I empty myself of thoughts, the fuller of God I am!

Aporia is Euporia. Emptiness of Being is fullness of Being.

I look across this parking lot of cars, traffic, houses and trees, full-bodied into God. I find myself to be *more like God* than these, to share more with God than with things.

They are like what we are; they are unlike.

And I know myself this day, writing in the autumn light, to be as immortal as It.

Once, spiritual knowledge was something eagerly sought for; now it is second nature to me and is much more to me than a set of theses though not verifiable in sense. *I see the spirit world.*

I have recognized spiritual knowledge as it came; it has only served to awaken deep memory.

I know, and I know that I know, that I am besouled and that my deep psyche/soul, uncluttered by the objects of sense, and the belief structures of the day, possesses knowledge of Being in its entirety, of realms seen and unseen.

Delphic Oracle: "Know thyself and thou shalt know God and the Universe."

"Spirit is not a fact to be taken over, it has to be learned." (Ludwig Edelstein)

You have to *turn the head.*

And then: You *see.*

I have felt inwardly apologetic to philosophy departments that I do not argue, except in *Earth Age* of which Calvin said he had never seen "so many and such complex arguments all designed to turn the head from its fixation with shadows on the wall."

You simply turn the head, and then you *see.*

When you make *this* Copernican Revolution in understanding Being, when you shift from taking matter to be the fundamental thing in the Universe and realize that consciousness is fundamental, then everything begins to make sense. And consciousness is not our thoughts, those sublimely coloured little birds flitting in and out of the aviary of our minds, but the dark spaces between thoughts, so like the night and so like cosmic space. Sometimes it is extended throughout our bodies, filled with the deep red energies of love, sometimes with light, incredible visions and images and strange remembrances, not of this life, but others and the world of spirit we all visit at night as our consciousness turns away from the physical and romps off into spiritual universes, at play.

These things I know.

The deep divine darkness of soul in which everything can be known.

I am an immortal being.

So are others.

So are cats and dogs and trees, a universe made by God and not by us.

They will all be there when we return to the realm of Spirit.

I hope—*I hope* that for the most part the things we human beings have fabricated, filled as they are with our consciousness, having to a limited extent a consciousness of their functions, will not be there.

"We dance our lives on deathless feet." (Frieda Lastrus) Now, the metaphysician puts down her pen.

Clive's dying, let it be our wake-up call, my brothers. Get in touch now with your heart's deepest desire for what you want to do in this life; the heart is where the will of God is given.

You know the terms of your contract here, as we all know.

Hope for all things, but that which thou lovest, that which you must do and would do, do it now and do not put it off.

As I grow older, among the beauties of the physical dimension of existence, the sweet rich green Earth and the starry universe, I savour fully the flavour of each day.

Give us this day.

My knowing is a function of the strange, enigmatic, pregnant-with-meaning words of others, which show their truth in the course of my lived life—"Oh that's what they meant!" Oh, now I see it—and a few central ideas not pruned away over time, remaining as distinguishing what is my own take from the vast sea of knowledge of our time (mainly more and more about less and less).

I realize that "starting" from Christianity and a path of prayer, I am at some place where Buddhists also are.

I am in a vast, untrammelled terrain, known by Intuition, a sure means of knowing.

What was unessential to the essence of Being has been stripped away.

I am in my period of late Matisse (hence the brevity of my expositions).

I knew, as a graduate student, in the mechanical interpretation of nature and the plurality of world-views, that when all is interpretation, philosophical attention must return to the interpreter whose interpretations they are—us, ourselves.

I thought *we* were the keys to the nature of the universe since we were in it and of it, part of it and therefore able to know it.

I thought that what happened "here" was related to what happened "there," that, together with Plato, things close to us that of themselves are less intelligible might be the keys to knowing what is far away from us but of itself more intelligible.

I felt that we knew truths of ethics with greater certainty than we knew the universe, and I made ethics the *touchstone* for testing, for verifying, world views or metaphysical theories. This was all done in my thesis.

And what was true?

That, or those, world-views—Oh for a glimpse of eternity, rather than views of the world, "a day on the threshold of your course, is better than a thousand elsewhere"—which accorded with ethics (Socrates' method as explained in Plato's *Phaedo*).

In my thesis (and book)—THE VERIFICATION OF METAPHYSICAL THEORIES: ETHICS AS BASIS FOR METAPHYSICS—those were the truths of the living God, God who cares for me, with whom one may enter into a relationship (barely glimpsed then) rather than the Cartesian Newtonian view of the world which dominates our age and in which I had grown up immersed and studied seriously at McGill and then at the graduate level.

Now I would say that ethics—respect for self and respect for others—is the tip of the iceberg of love and is given by the heart. Mind and its ideas must bow to the heart having its own "reasons which reason doth not know." (Pascal)

"Reason climbs a ladder up to love and then it must lay down its weapons and serve." (Catharine Dougherty)

And I would say that reality communicates itself to us more fully through the emotions than to the mind.

Faith is not belief. It simply is "knowledge born of love," "...knowledge born of love rather than mind." (Bernard Lonergan)

But so my way has been: To take ourselves, and our inner beings—we are the only beings in the universe to which we have access to the inner side of the universe, which Teilhard de Chardin called "the within"—as keys to the true nature of the universe.

In a nutshell?

The universe is like us; we are like the universe.

It has been a long journey from the chaotic beliefs of the modern world to this simple city by the sea under grey skies (and full of puddles reflecting trees and sky in which, as Virginia Woolf put it, mystics find some little thing that they are seeking and which satisfies their souls).

There is a journey into that distance, that distinct and whole way of knowing that the sages called "not knowing." I now think that God is all that can be known. We know God in ourselves, for we are fragments of God, we know God in the ground under our feet, for Earth is full of God, and we know God directly, gaze into gaze, beyond the world of things and beings. For God and ourselves are like, very very like, and God is not, as the theologians have said, "wholly other." God is near; God is close, very close "in our hearts and on our lips."

There are only two kinds of being in the universe. One is God formless; the other is God in form, i.e. ourselves and the world. With God, we can fully commune, inner to inner, soul to soul.

The One who is.

The tremendous energy from which we all spring.

I take time in a busy day to connect with Spirit. Then I go forth, to live fully here, as one day I shall live there. God often addresses us through the words of others; perhaps all knowledge is really revelation.

This: We *see* it, as one can see ideas, and the other who finally sees also can say yes it is so. All insights are really revelatory of the ways the nature of that which "loves to hide" (Heraclitus) reveals itself.

I cannot commend enough to all the beauty of the Earth, for beauty is as Plato said the one form which shines *here* as it shines *there,* and when you are enraptured with the beauty of the Earth, you are gazing into God.

Now I go to be with the grey Saturday, to see what doings are afoot, in my little city by the sea. A great barrier has come down this day, an inner barrier yields. From now on, I shall say what I *know* to be true. May I jog your memories!

How is it possible to take off the blinkers? Because we have a spirit which is not of the world around us, which can distance itself from what happens.

I even like cars when they take me to you, or to the country, and warm houses in winter.

It was ethics turned my head in the modern cave. In a world of facts, where does anything you "ought to do" come from?

Sydney, September, 1999

6.

Of Plato and the Ideas

For Michael, "He who is loved by God"
"Endure my heart; thou hath born worst things than these"
                                                          —Odysseus

Divinest Plato.

In that civilization so intensely aware of the beauty of the human form, Plato understood love better than anyone. He was the first philosopher, and the last, to write of it.

The Symposium. The lesser mysteries—behind all begetting of off-spring is a yearning for the eternal. The greater mysteries—the begetting of works of art, constitutions of cities and states, up, up, up, passing from one beauty in existence to another, to a vision of the Forms themselves, the eternal and unchanging patterns against which the Earth and all her inhabitants, and the cosmos itself, were fashioned.

And from this vision?

One returned to the ordinary world, to practise virtue, which is what it is to live "timeless as mortal man may." (Socrates)

Love seeks the eternal in all its ways of manifesting itself. "Bringing to birth in beauty, offspring, works of art, virtue."

The true end of love is the eternal, the Forms themselves.

Reason has the same true end as love, the eternal, the Forms. These, reason attains through the art of *dialectic*, reason's continual critique of its own first premises. Hegel: "Consciousness suffers death at its own hands, flying upwards from one first principle to another as up a flight of stairs until argument and first principles are left behind and reason beholds the Forms themselves."

Love and reason both seek the eternal, both lead through proper discipline to a vision of the unchanging patterns and therefore to the very foundations of the world.

There are corollaries:

Virtue is knowledge. There is a Form for the virtues—the virtues of courage, wisdom, temperance—justice, which both love and reason can grasp.

Knowledge is virtue. When you know what the true nature of reality is, you will live virtuously.

And so, Plato gave us the concept of the well-ordered, tripartite soul—reason, the passions, the spirited part. With the soul, virtue moves from an outward to an inner sphere. From the well-ordered soul, virtuous acts proceed.

(I keep mine ordered through prayer.)

The Form; the Ideas.

Plato was right; there are Ideas behind the universe we see.

And the simile of the cave is an accurate picture of human existence.

Briefly: Human beings live in an underground cave, chained by their necks so that they can see only the wall before them.

A fire lit behind them casts their shadows on the wall. They take these shadows to be Reality and compete for prizes in measuring their motion.

(Modern Science. I know it well.)

At one side of the cave, a stairway leads to the world above where there are trees and people and animals walking around, and clouds in the sky, and the splendid silent sun itself.

Now, if someone were to come down into this cave and unchain the inhabitants and turn their heads, show them the fire and lead them up the stairs and into the light of day, they would be utterly amazed.

At first they would be blind until their eyes became accustomed to the light, but then they would make out the people and animals and trees. They would see the sun, the author of all things, and begin to understand the true nature of reality and to realize how mistaken they were to think the shadows on the wall were *"really* Real."

(For me, it was Kant's ethics which undid my chains and turned my head, leading as it does to an entirely different view of the world than the scientific view with which I had grown up. But this is a long story and I have told it elsewhere.)

So Plato draws a distinction between Appearance and Reality.

The shadows on the wall of the cave are "appearances" of something "more real" above.

The world we *take* to be the Real, the everyday world of tables and chairs, cats and dogs, is not ultimately real at all but a shadow of something *more* Real.

For Plato, the world of changing being could not have any ultimate reality, that belongs to unchanging being, the Ideas, the Forms. Only the Forms, the Ideas, were *really* Real.

How appropriate it is then that all the dialogues culminate in *aporia*, contradictions and uncertainties, which prepare the way for deeper questions and the next dialogue.

The same thing happens in modern science at the *limits*—the very small, the very fast, the very large, the very far away. Cartesian/Newtonian science was fine for the ordinary world of our experience, and then, as it transcended the boundaries of that world, it ran into contradictions and concluded, as do Plato's dialogues, that the world is not ultimately real. The universe is something more.

So evolved Plato's way of reason—from things "close to us but of themselves less intelligible" to things "far from us but of themselves more intelligible."

The Ideas, the Forms.

These are not the only elements of Plato's *Real*.

There is also the *One* which is the ultimate source of being, and the Good, which is "beyond being."

Could we not say, as has been said, that the One is God, source of all being, and the Good is the value of existence itself, all being realized and perpetuated in "value fulfilment," love and joy?

How does creation come to be?

How is the universe formed?

Plato needed a half God, the demiurge, who, using the Forms as patterns or blueprints would, like a master builder, translate them into existence. Of themselves, the Ideas could do nothing; they needed a translator.

The task of the demiurge was to "persuade matter," which was simply lying about, to cooperate with the patterns of the Forms and make a universe. Matter is very unruly stuff, which is why things go wrong and accidents happen. It had never been quite fully persuaded to form a cosmos.

Plato knew well the scientific accounts of the universe of his time, the "chance and necessity" universe of Anaxagoras which is the same as the modern account.

He contrasted the scientific account with his own view—that the universe came into being "by Art" or "by design,"—and he thought that it made a great difference in human affairs whether people believed in one theory or the other.

Essentially: The scientific versus the religious account of reality. It is all there in Plato. How was he able to see and to truly see so much?

Plato's inspiration was Pythagorean geometry, with its eternal squares, triangles and circles.

Aristotle's inspiration was biology and the arts. He took Plato's forms and set them in motion *in* the world, an eternal element appearing *within* changing being.

For some learned physicists, scientific laws were the ideas in the mind of God. That was a reconciliation of sorts of science and religion.

But since then?

Cartesian science, modern science, has gone one way, religious thought another, and quantum physics yet a third.

It is time for a new synthesis.

I shall attempt it here, and I will bring into my synthesis the Forms, the Ideas. Deepak Chopra makes such a synthesis, but he reduces the entire universe to vibration and that is the account of modern physics.

For modern physics, the universe is vibrations, and what we call the real world, the ordinary world of our lives, arises as the vibrations of the universe impinge on the vibrations which are our brains.

But such an account ends by reducing the whole of reality to vibrations, with consciousness appearing at the end.

I shall begin with consciousness as the essential stuff of the universe. The universe originated from a loving "sea of consciousness, criss-crossed by vibrations."

Vibrations differ in frequency but they all have "intent" as does *all consciousness*. Like-vibrations dance together to see what they can produce. Indeed "like attracts like" is a deep law of all of Being. They dance together, they play to see what they can "make."

(I use quotation marks here because we can only speak metaphorically about these things. They are really beyond our capacity to know.)

Bundles of like vibrations form Ideas.

Ideas are thus patterns, intermediaries and organizing principles between us and the infinite vibrations of the universe.

Ideas are endowed with consciousness and with an intent and capability to "manifest" themselves. It is from the ideas that all of reality we know—waking and sleeping, visible and invisible—comes.

Ideas are thus intermediaries between the "sea of consciousness" with its vibrations and the physical/spiritual universe.

The Ideas.

They are Real.

They are intermediaries between spirit and us.

But they are not what Plato thought they were. They require no demiurge to translate them, nor are they endlessly unchanging. Ideas change! Witness the world.

They manifest themselves.

Ideas are endowed with consciousness and the intent to manifest. They are highly animate beings, the intelligence of the universe.

Ideas are formed of masses of vibrations; when the vibrations are "dense enough," they appear solid. There are ideas of everything—units of consciousness, fundamental particles, molecules, beings, trees, plants, people and stars.

It is *the interplay of Ideas* that form all of creation, visible and invisible, physical and spiritual. We shall speak of the physical first.

"How" you may say, can a harmonious universe, a cosmos rather than a chaos, result from such an arrangement?

The universe is like a dance floor where every one is moving smoothly to the music. The dance will only be interrupted by an outside influence, say somebody under the influence of alcohol.

But in the universe, *there are no "outside" influences.*

There are only Ideas, dense or less dense, sending out vibrations in all directions, interacting with one another, a tremendous field of vibrations, complex, but not complicated. Ideas are patterns, and they project themselves outwards, as images on a film are projected onto a screen.

Only—and this is the mystery of the universe, which is not about to be assimilated to mechanism—what are the ideas projected onto?

There is no screen.

The motive powers of the world lie in the Ideas, the true inner of things which are endowed with consciousness and intent. Truly, we live our lives in the shadow of ideas.

And now, five questions:

> How do the Ideas which form the universe relate to ideas in our minds?
>
> How do the precise mathematical order of the universe, and the laws of nature, and the forces arise?
>
> What about development? How does the Idea that forms the plant relate to the idea of the genetic code? What is really happening in development?
>
> What is going on in evolution?
>
> Where and what is spirit in all of this?

First, ideas in our minds are just like ideas in the universe, simply in a more compact version. They are not produced by the brain. The brain is like an antenna which picks up vibrations sent out by ideas in nature.

How does the idea, for example, of a plant get within our minds?

The idea that manifests as a certain plant is always sending out vibrations. These vibrations are picked up by our antenna brains, and recognized as that plant, as that idea. *There are profound mass agreements of all kinds on the nature of physical reality that we have all made before coming here.*

Aristotle thought that in a way "the soul becomes all things." That does happen in a way; the ideas we have of the plant derive from the idea that is forming a plant, but it is not exactly the same. There is distortion in the system. There is a relation between the two ideas. The universe is essentially formed by interplay among ideas, a dance of Forms but not of things.

The senses are "lovely liars." (Seth) The world of solidity and colour, taste and sound is a camouflage over the Real.

So Socrates, as a lover of wisdom, saw in death a possible release from his confinement to sense and also saw the possibility of knowing truly what was what.

Saint Paul: Here we see in a glass darkly, but there face to face. Now we know in part; there we shall know even as we are known.

Of my *second* question: How do we understand the breathtakingly beautiful, precise mathematical order of the universe?

F=ma. Two billiard balls collide, with a force that is equal to their mass times their acceleration. Physics books are full of such mathematical equations.

I want to suggest, that such interactions are a complex interaction of many ideas and sub ideas, and that the mathematical order itself is such an idea, powerfully informing both the universe and our minds, and simply put, is the simplest possible kind of order. To ask why is this is the order of the universe is to ask why a baby crawls before it walks. As for precision, I suspect there are much more complex kinds of order, and that most of reality is missed by physic's text books.

The universe of space, time and matter is really a limited "set of rules of the game" for our existence here and the existence of the physical universe, whereas really all is happening simultaneously. Mathematics describes only the very surface of what is really going on, despite all its elegance.

Third, what of the biological question of, for example, the development of a plant?

Again, many complex ideas and sub-ideas interact. If this sounds vague, I am not being evasive. I do not know how else to say it.

Fourth, of evolution: Are evolutionary premises, chance mutation and natural selection, an account of how more complex forms emerge from simple ones?

What is often missed in the evolutionary account is the creative interplay between spiritual and physical worlds and the power of ideas to manifest.

But I am dealing with reality so far beyond the power of words to describe that it can be barely glimpsed in meditation. All I say must be taken metaphorically. The spiritual world is a world, a realm, in which

Oneness prevails, very different from the separated state of the physical world.

For the *fifth* question: Where is spirit in all of this?

Spirit is everywhere, an "idea so powerful that it is within and affects every other idea." Spirit gives rise to the sea of consciousness and every other reality. How? Why? These questions are so far beyond our ability that we must call it mystery. How can we speak at all of that universe in which everything is happening simultaneously in the terms which are appropriate for space, time and matter and yet are not merely the rules of the game?

One thing is clear. The world around us is for the most part an illusion, colours, sound. This world that is truly so real to us—our physical world in space and time—arises as an interaction between ourselves and ideas.

Materialists are fond of reducing the mind to the brain. The mind is but an epiphenomenon, they say. As William James put it for them: "It is like the shadow which runs beside the runner without influencing his stride."

The truth is: The whole universe of matter is the real epiphenomenon, a mere cork bobbing on the ocean of spirit, on the spiritual reality of Ideas.

Does all this sound bizarre?

It isn't. Quantum physics has reduced everything to vibration or has reduced matter to vibration. All it needs to do is understand that there is a deeper organization in ideas, inn fact, an order something like that suggested by David Bohm with his theory of implicate order.

Plato was *essentially* correct. How much he saw. How much they saw, those first philosophers, dwelling as they did so close to Being, more directly in contact with what can be known.

As for the ideas I have presented here, one cannot think them. In deep meditation one may glimpse the reality whereof I speak.

*   *   *

Modern physics has reduced the entire universe to "vibrations."

Vibrations of what?

Vibrations of energy.

But the flip side of energy is consciousness: All energy has consciousness, all consciousness has energy. The universe comes to be from spirit, infinite consciousness, eternal and imperishable—the most powerful idea of all.

Ideas are intermediaries between spirit and the universe as it were, though spirit is in each one and affects each one. Truly there is nothing but spirit, infinite love-consciousness, at play with itself, ramifying into millions of different forms and into each of us. Formed and formless, we are spirit's offspring, the intelligence of the universe in ideas and in spirit which affects ideas, for we have free will but are being carefully guided all the time. For the sake of our limited understanding, we might diagram these as follows:

Spirit
Ideas
The Physical Universe
Us

What is most crucial to remember in all of this is that the vibrations, and the bundles of like vibrations we can call ideas whose interplay gives rise to the universe—unlike Plato's ideas—have consciousness. Consciousness is the decisive U-turn in our metaphysics and for a very different universe from that described as the "chance and necessity" mechanical universe. The universe is formed from Infinite Consciousness; that is the stuff of the universe, love-consciousness at that, organized into ideas which come and go.

Matter, lustrous and beautiful as it is, is not "really Real." It is the true epiphenomenon here. The stars are ciphers to the greater whole; matter arises at the interface between the Ideas and us. Laslo was right: We are all climbing higher and higher in the "mountainous territory of being and eternity."

That is what the universe really is.

And so for a new Plato. You will know, Michael, what to make of all this.

We are indeed "such stuff as dreams are made of and our little life is rounded with a sleep." We can know anything in the vast physical and spiritual universe—God's dream. The only things that really matter in this universe of consciousness that are really worthwhile are love *and* being fully alive.

This is not the universe of Newton. This is not even the universe of Einstein—space, time, matter and light. It is beyond both. It is a universe which has been truly glimpsed by religious men and women, scientists and philosophers. It has a place for all; it is time to let the barriers between us down. It is a universe rich, complex, creative and wise beyond all telling. Our ordinary world is an appearance, but it is an appearance of something. It is an appearance especially in the natural beauty of the Earth, of a *reality rare, radiant and fathomless, and of our own true natures which are indeed "very, very like."*

Plato had most of it in embryonic form, and truly, the philosophical thinkers of the west really are a series of footnotes to Plato. (Whitehead)

Finally, Plato was right about love, about having "another half" which we are constantly in search of. How good the universe is. Truly, love will prevail over every darkness. At the dawn of creation, when each of us embarked upon our own cosmic journey, each of us was created with the other half, like ourselves, so very, very like, but opposite.

When life becomes overwhelming, I remind myself that my twin flame waits in the world of spirit. When this life is over, what stories I shall return to share. For now? What God said to Moses is true: "Go on!"

So much for the Ideas; we live in their shadow. Yet now I remember that St. John of Cross says that on the path to prayer "one idea remaining in the mind is enough to keep God out." And I remember that St. Teresa says: "He who has God ceases to want; God alone suffices." But now the golden sun of October is streaming down on dark seas. Oh God, I will take the grey clouds, the sun over ideas any day. And Ideas.

Knowing that we live in a universe that is conscious, intelligent throughout, a fit home for us and all creatures, created in love for the well-being of all, emergent through creative play, how can our lives not be about joy and adventure here? Now, bring ideas to Earth and embody them. Whoever thought of the idea of water or fire, rain, wind and snow; this is the real mystery. Do we have to claim our ordinary world as a mere illusion? Seth: "A clever camouflage; the senses are lovely liars." Illusion? I say magic, for its beauty is carried upon the spirit of God which can touch us from any corner of creation.

So I shall go on loving the fall colours, the dark seas, the white-capped waves, knowing there is something there, and I shall craft them into form. Knowing, if all things pass and this be but a dance of vibrations, I shall still love it ardently. Beauty cannot be explained away. The real mysteries begin the other side of Cartesian geometry, and the Shaman is one who works with the deep consciousness, energy, patterns. Buddha possessed this sense of reality and merely called it "suchness." Our task he thought was not suchness but to work on ourselves in a world of suchness. What is our task here? To bring powerful concepts to civilization which may guide it into its most invigorating future. To bring Ideas to Earth. Nothing is more powerful for human beings than ideas.

Forms, Ideas, and the joys of sense.

We live our lives in the shadow of Ideas.

Let them only bring us more fully to Earth.

Rilke: Show him things...(*Elegies*)

Rilke: Here should we live, amidst Infinities?
       Show him daily an honest, confident task done
       Guide him close to the garden
       Give him the counterbalancing nights
       Withhold him...

Peace Michael
October, 1999

7.

Laws of the Universe

For Len, "Ari Ben David"
"I come that you may have life and have it to the full."

We all have free will.

We come from God; we shall return to God; we yearn for God, as God once yearned for us.

Reincarnation is the way the Universe works because the laws of love are ultimate; justice prevails and it needs time and space for its out-working.

We choose the major circumstances of our own lives before birth; we chose our parents for what we shall learn from them, and we *co-create* everything that happens to us on the Earth plane.

We choose our destinies. Our only limits are spiritual ignorance.

We have major life lessons to be learned here of which love and joy in the physical plane are the most important. Love, joy and wisdom are the will of God for us here. All the laws of the universe are ultimately derivative from principles of consciousness and love-consciousness at that.

God has been revealed as unconditional love in every system of reality.

*   *   *

God is unconditional love.

We are fine just as we are, perfect as we are.

Accept the whole of yourself.

Religions are all in disarray right now because of their notions of what we are all supposed to look like, given the reality of God. They are full of strive! strive! strive! Our religions are too limited to contain our own true nature and they are giving way. We have a shadow side as well as a light side, and the unrest and upheaval in the world right now are not just the passing away of an old age but are the direct result of burying our shadow sides and projecting them on another.

We are not meant to be perfect.

We are not meant to be good or perfect, just whole.

Unconditional love is all that is important, accepting of ourselves and others, tolerant and embracing of our differences.

When you take the world of spirit seriously, it will take you seriously.

There are three laws of the human universe. They are *intent*, *attraction* and *allowing*.

Intent enables you to co-create your reality and the reality of the world with God, here on the Earth plane, to form a clear idea of what you want—what your deepest self wants is the will of God—and to state it with love and emotion to the universe. Then let it go. This is to inform the great universe of consciousness and get it behind you. Goethe: When you form a clear idea of what you want to achieve, everything falls into place, the right books, the right people.

The next law is *attraction*. People who are like you will be drawn to you with the chance to play together and see what it is possible to make.

Allowing: Allow yourself to be who you are and allow others to be. All are at various stages through life's journey. Every one is unique, an embodiment of different belief structures.

Pray and help will come immediately from the spiritual world.

You are never given more than you can handle.

Know your cup and drink it.

God brings good out of everything for those who love him. "Eye hath not seen, nor ear heard, nor has it entered into the heart of man, what God has prepared for those who love him."

Scripture is sound when it comes from love, not fear.

Sydney, NS
Autumn

8.

The Metaphysician Puts Down Her Pen

(To go to be with the day)

Dedicated to Peter Poole
"Lo, no man knows
Through what wild centuries
Roves back the rose."
—The Wandering Scholars (Helen Waddell)

What follows from all this?

A new conception of the universe, yet very ancient, both Platonic and Aristotelian, Kantian and Hegelian, put forward in very simple terms by my mind, body, soul and spirit which, in all the learning of our age, has taken that path mapped out by the muses of Form. I have followed both the needs of my own nature for unity and the richness of my own Pisces soul with its tendency to take in absolutely everything.

Essentially the universe has evolved out of love, joy and creative play and is permeated with wisdom and intelligence, indeed a green dragon.

As Brian Swimme put it: Chance, necessity and mechanism, have their places within it…but it encompasses them, not they it.

The universe, being essentially consciousness, functioning under purposefulness, is essentially *more like us than we have ever dared dream possible.*

For Newton and Laplace: Physics; God? "Sire, I have no need of that hypothesis."

For James Jeans, astronomer, the universe was "more like a vast thought than a vast machine."

For me it is living, conscious, spiritual and divine and is like the Earth which is also living, conscious, spiritual and divine. It is like unto myself; the Earth and the universe are like us. Perhaps we may feel at home here now that the barriers are down. We felt very alone when we thought we were the only being which had reason and thought, which functioned by plans and purposes. Now we may be at home here and care for the Earth as we care for ourselves.

Perhaps now we can relax.

God is unconditional love.

We are fragments of such.

Love is the value, like Plato's good which permeates the whole, and has formed a universe hospitable to every being within it, including us.

We belong here.

All the news is good.

Let us bring heaven to Earth, spirit here, our spirituality to Earth and truly be alive here. Enjoy and write works that will teach us to dance.

I am in *awe* of the astounding marvellousness of it all. With Kant: The starry heavens above me, the moral law within me, with the whole of creation and the spirit within it.

Indeed, beauty *is* for Plato, and for me too, the one form that shines "here" as it does "there," and it is beauty which for a soul sensitive to such enables me to write. Writing is a form for me of the love of God. Now I see people and cars and trees again and there are clouds floating above, and the sun shines through on the sea and here in Tim Horton's people are drinking coffee and reading the morning paper. How grateful I am for the ordinary world, the day just going on, the passage of time and "the beauties of our lives." (Ken Henwood)

How have I written this?

Truly, reverence for the beauty of my male friends puts me in mind of the God in heaven we have all followed and reminds me of the things of heaven. Love and respect are indeed "principles of knowing." And you *ground* me.

What else follows from this account?

I think now, women may find the universe a hospitable place to be, and also find a new model for civilization on the Earth plane, up till now formed on the model of mechanics, in likeness to the true, the good and the beautiful, a civilization in balance with the Earth and hospitable to every being on the Earth plane. They really do not feel quite at home in mechanical worlds. We like dance and play, lightness, the informal, the natural.

A little less attention to "grave duty."

I foresee a new richness, a new flowering. Love (women's principle) and reason (the male principle) seek the same ends—a way of living here which is as timeless as mortal beings may.

That way of living is joy.

Now I really do put down my pen. I have written my multiplicity into a unity and am ravelled up "free of thoughts" (pesky creatures that they are and general disturbers of the peace), and I am whole once again—One!

What else follows from my account?

The key is that consciousness is the very most essential stuff of the universe, that all true explanatory principles lay within it and that we are the keys to the nature of the whole.

What follows I leave for each person to work out for themselves in their own way. Consider that all our limitations come from spiritual ignorance and that the term to connect with reality is "consciousness." I am certain that simply knowing the truth about reality cannot fail to affect us. "Philosophy is the guardian of the soul." (Plato)

This account cannot fail to affect our lives here because Plato was right: Knowledge is virtue.

What I have written has wide implications for the way we relate to each other and the Earth. For the rest?

I do not know.

You must ask Plato.

Now I suspect the universe has had enough of me pestering it. The true nature of things loves to hide (Heraclitus), so I shall go for a walk and a talk with God, among the ducks and the trees of Wentworth Pond. The singing heart is the guide to life. "In him there is nothing to fear, he is only loveable." (Eckhart)

I Am, Lorna Green, Mystic
September, 1999

9.

My Place in the Scheme of Things

For Graham: "Love is Eternal"
—Abraham Lincoln

Life is about healing and wholeness.

The universe unfolds as my apartment has unfolded here, and comes to order, order of a loose kind, appropriate to an intuitive. It is a large, spacious, two-bedroom apartment which gets the morning sun. It is carpeted throughout with sandy-coloured carpet, clean white walls, smoky-rose Venetian blinds, a few green plants, a dark green card table with a tall rose-coloured candle on it and a white lamp, a lazy boy reclining armchair, and a wooden rocking chair—that is for the living room. In the spacious clean kitchen, a small white oval kitchen table with two chairs, many green plants, another rose-coloured candle.

The first bedroom empty, save for a few boxes. The back room, looking into trees, has a full mattress on the floor, covered with sheets and a green woven blanket, a small dark wooden structure and yet another tall rose-coloured candle—these candles do get lit—and the card of a late Matisse—his blue exuberant female form with flying arms on a white background.

Those are the essentials, the basics, the Forms. The first to arrive in my apartment at 503 Charlotte Street—my house during all my growing up years was 503 Fraser Avenue—were the wooden rocking chairs, the green candle, the green card table and my four tote bags containing a few clothes and some manuscripts (the universe is meant to travel). (This was the time to separate myself from my mother who died last winter, to integrate inner mother.)

Next came two potted plants, two green ceramic cereal bowls, several knives, forks and spoons, and paring knife, one can opener (the universe has the basics in hand, the forms).

The first Form—three coffee mugs from a nun friend, the most important things. One has a seagull (which my father always wanted to be in the after life) and says on its side: "I do my best and then leave the rest to God."

So, among these basics, I rocked and brooded and talked with God, and assimilated my new surroundings, and made brief forays out into Sydney, the bank (for abundance) the post office (for letters to friends), the nearest cafe, Tim Horton's for writing.

I allowed myself a long time to assimilate my new reality—the universe is patient, slow; it takes its time, which enables it to realize fully the potential of the beginning.

Gradually, over time, a few green plants came, the candles, some inexpensive second-hand furniture (the universe makes do). Elegant, simple, beautiful.

Now?

The energy in those bags has spawned piles of file folders for ideas, poetry, writing, business (a plain cardboard box contains this summer's note books). Oh, a white phone came for long-distance communication (the universe harmonizes and integrates all aspects of itself).

Now, two bottles of pure spring water are here, a small upright vacuum cleaner, clothes draped over the rocking chair, a couple of pairs of shoes, loosely arranged, the card table bearing a shaman painting, a picture of two sea otters cuddled together, a photo of a native girl, an engraved postcard of the 23rd psalm, "The Lord is my shepherd, I shall not want." *Desiderata,* from Graham, is in my back room on the wooden stand, along with a few books for spiritual reading.

My desk is covered with and also contains white index cards with advice, which I sometimes take. The kitchen has one silver pot and one silver Teflon frying pan, a spatula, a slotted spoon.

The refrigerator is well-stocked with yogurt, vegetables, wheat germ, fruit and a little meat in the freezer for grounding.

On the counter is some All Bran (the universe is sensible about the fundamentals), a bag of raw oats, some bananas, some bottles of vitamin pills. My apartment also contains a lovely small bathroom, tiled in rose with green bath mats and towels.

Now the picture is complete. That is the modern world. I have an am/fm radio, for *occasional news,* and a switch which flips from classical music to modern/western.

It has come together one step at a time with the slowly emerging order firmed up by white cards on the card table desk, my sense of identity. Precise order and chaos come and go rather like the tides. I tidy the room and then a few pieces of paper appear, straying out from piles and gradually it is chaos. I hang up the clothes and they gradually reappear draped over the rocking chair. That is how it is with an intuitive. Ash once said of me that "reality arranges itself." (May it be so in small and great ways.) I am completely at home in what to other people approximates total disorder, but in that state I know exactly where everything is, and that is true.

Well, that is exactly how the universe is, pulsing, going in and out of existence, firming up, ravelling out, contracting and expanding, sometimes beautiful to behold, sometimes such a mess that one must go out on Saturday just to be out of it. One never quite knows what to do on Sundays.

My apartment has a storage room for old things, and an empty room for new things. Here is where I live in God, casually, loosely, at home in my own soul, living in the deep waters of my own unconscious, interfacing with the world for business. That is how the universe is and it, too, knows not quite what to do with itself on Sunday.

My apartment is the ocean in which a Pisces soul finds its way in all the different energies and is at home.

(The carpet tends to accumulate loose change and paper clips).

All peace.
Sydney, NS
Autumn

Epilogue

...ays for nine brother adventurers in Being,
...mber of the divine (3x3).

A Carmelite
...ays every debt."

...a life? *A spirit is tempered.*

Peace, Lorna

November, 1999

Photo by Janet Green Foster, 2002

Author's Biography

Lorna Green was born in Ottawa, Canada, on February 28, 1939, in a snowstorm. She spent her teen-age years canoeing the Ottawa River.

She studied science (BSc McGill University, Montreal; PhD, The Rockefeller University, New York 1965) in the conviction that science could explain the universe. When she discovered it could not—all scientific explanations rest on "unexplained explainers"—she turned to the study of philosophy for answers (MA, University of Toronto; PhD thesis undefended, published as ETHICS AS BASIS FOR META-PHYSICS) and especially to ethics. Where, in a world of facts, does anything one "ought" to do come from?

While teaching the Great Books at St. Johns College in Santa Fe, New Mexico, a student told her of a monastery in the mountains she "must visit." It was the Benedictine and charismatic monastery of Pecos, New Mexico. She went, and knew at once by the Joy on the faces of the men and women in community there that they had the truth she was seeking. There, in the world of dreams, ethics, which she had made the touchstone for Metaphysics, opened out into God and charismatic Catholicism—she simply stepped into the living waters of the Love that God is. She teaches and writes from this base.

At the age of forty, she returned to Canada, married her long time friend Don Knight, and took up a wilderness life of prayer, writing and practical tasks in Canada's maritime province of Nova Scotia. There, all her learning came together.

Since the age of twenty-one, she had wanted to write Metaphysics. She began to know what was what when she was forty-eight and made her second pass at Metaphysics in EARTH AGE: A NEW VISION OF GOD, THE HUMAN AND THE EARTH (Paulist Press, 1994). She has been writing Metaphysics ever since because we really cannot be happy without knowing the nature of Reality.

She now lives in the great desert of the Southwest..

She is sixty-three.

A true Canadian understands winter.

0-595-26493-X